MOUNTAIN BIKING
Santa Monica Mountains'
BEST TRAILS

By Jim Hasenauer
& Mark Langton

MOUNTAIN
BIKING
PRESS™

FINE EDGE
Productions

IMPORTANT LEGAL NOTICE AND DISCLAIMER

Credits:
book design: Melanie Haage
copy editing: Réanne Hemingway-Douglass & Cindy Kamler
diagrams: Sue Irwin, Faith Rumm
cover photos: © Mark Langton
all other photos by the authors, except as noted

Library of Congress Cataloging-in-Publication Data

Hasenauer, Jim, 1949–
    Mountain biking the Santa Monica Mountains' best trails / by Jim Hasenauer and Mark Langton.
        p.   cm.
    Includes bibliographical references and index.
    ISBN 0-938665-55-3
    1. All terrain cycling--California--Santa Monica Mountains--Guidebooks.   2. All terrain vehicle trails--California--Santa Monica Mountains--Guidebooks.   3. Santa Monica Mountains (Calif.)--Guidebooks.   I. Langton, Mark.   II. Title.
GV1045.5.C22S344   1998   98-23023
796.6'3'09794--dc21   CIP

ISBN ISBN 0-938665-55-3

Address requests for permission to
Mountain Biking Press™
Fine Edge Productions, Route 2, Box 303, Bishop, CA 93514
www.fineedge.com

ACKNOWLEDGMENTS

Christie Logan put up with a generally distracted, specifically fixated partner for several months. I owe you several hours of computer time. And more. My bicycling comrades from the CORBA Steering Committee—Peter Heumann, Matt Landis, Mark Langton, Kurt Loheit and Lou Pescarmona—have become good friends. They were not only supportive throughout this project, but they willingly covered my lessened involvement in our land access work as I pushed toward deadline. Roger Piper, Aaron Cox and Victor Vincente provided important background information as I traced the history of bicycles in the Santa Monica Mountains. Tom Robbins, Elayne Haggan and many other riders were helpful in suggesting rides that I hadn't tried. I did, and they're in here. Don and Réanne Douglass and Sue Irwin of Fine Edge Productions were alternatively supportive, helpful, insisting, rigorous and rewarding. Thanks, I needed that.

—Jim Hasenauer

* * *

In the nearly 25 years that I have been recreating in the Santa Monica Mountains, I have seen great change. Many acres have been lost to development, but many have been saved as well, thanks to the hard work of such organizations as the Santa Monica Mountains Trails Council and Save Open Space. As well, each and every person who has volunteered his or her time to protect and preserve the public parks within the Santa Monica Mountains National Recreation Area is to be commended. Without these people, we might not have the parks for future generations.

In nearly 11 years of mountain biking advocacy, I have seen even greater change. When I first began riding mountain bikes in the Santa Monica Mountains in 1983, I could identify who had ridden there before me by their tire tracks. Now, on any given weekend, there are thousands of mountain bikers enjoying our public trails. I would like to thank all of those cyclists whose behavior we can hold up as an example of responsible riding; it is you who allow us continued access to the trails.

I would like to thank all of those who have joined the Concerned Off-Road Bicyclists Association to help spread the word of responsible cycling. This especially goes for all those who have served as volunteer patrol members of the Mountain Biking Unit, or who have ever participated in trail building and maintenance. Thanks to you, the mountain bike community is the most well organized of all recreational groups and has contributed more hours than all other volunteer groups combined. It is because of you that this guide can exist.

Lastly, I would like to thank my wife Teresa for putting up with all the late nights and lost weekends researching this guide. Her support and love are a continual inspiration.

—Mark Langton

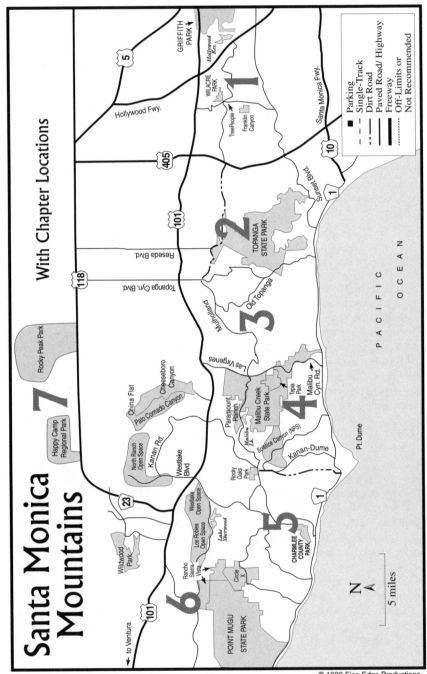

Santa Monica Mountains

With Chapter Locations

N

5 miles

© 1998 Fine Edge Productions

FOREWORD

In January of 1996, several bicyclists gathered at the southeast end of the Backbone Trail in Will Rogers State Historic Park. The six-mile Rogers Road section of the Backbone, a singletrack which climbs steeply into Topanga State Park, was being re-opened to mountain bicyclists after being closed for nine years. It was a great day. Most days spent mountain biking in the Santa Monicas are great days.

A lot has happened in the mountains since the first edition of this guidebook appeared in 1989, and most of it has been good for mountain bicyclists. The Concerned Off-Road Bicyclists Association (CORBA) and the International Mountain Bicycling Association (IMBA) have both gained strength and credibility in representing responsible mountain bicyclists. Many once-closed trails are now open to bikes. (However, several miles of trails are still closed. It is the continued responsible riding habits of all cyclists that will allow more of these trails to become available.)

The National Park Service, California State Parks, The Santa Monica Mountains Conservancy and the Conejo Open Space Conservation Agency, the four large public land managers in the Santa Monicas, have maintained successful land acquisition and trail construction programs. As these new parks and trails came on-line, most of them have been opened to bicycles.

Some things haven't changed at all. The Santa Monicas are still unbelievably beautiful. Whether you're toodling along with your family or on a long-distance technical adventure, the trails of the Santa Monicas offer stunning views, a changing palette of native plants, a surprising number of encounters with wildlife, and the chance to leave urban Los Angeles far behind. A bike ride here is regenerative. It nourishes body, mind and spirit.

The seasonal changes are subtle here, but if you visit often enough, you'll become familiar with them. Winter rains fill streams, and waterfalls gush and then disappear as summer comes on. The spring green turns to gold then gray as winter nears. There's a succession of wildflower bloom beginning with those first rains and lasting late into fall. With the exception of avoiding muddy, rain-soaked trails in the winter and respecting the ominous fire danger and park closures when the Santa Anas blow, you can ride all year here.

I believe that bikes belong on the Santa Monica Mountains trails and that shared-use trails offer the most opportunities for the most park visitors. In this "Bikes Belong—Share the Trails" vision, bicyclists take on a special obligation to prove ourselves. Please follow the IMBA Rules of the Trail. Expect and respect other trail users. Do your part to contribute to the future of mountain biking.

Welcome to the Santa Monicas. If you don't know yet, you will come to know how precious they are, and how threatened they are by urban encroachment. Be their champion. Mark and I will see you on the trails.

—Jim Hasenauer

Contents

Acknowledgments   *3*

Santa Monica Mountains Area Map with Chapter Locations   *4*

Foreword   *5*

Introduction   *9*

A Brief History of Mountain Biking in the Santa Monicas   *14*

Special Considerations   *18*

1   **The Eastern Santa Monicas**   *21*
      Griffith Park; Lake Hollywood Reservoir; Cross Mountain Park—
      TreePeople, Franklin Canyon and Wilacre Park
      MAP: Franklin Canyon/TreePeople/Wilacre Park   *24*

2   **Sepulveda Pass to Topanga Canyon**   *27*
      East Side Dirt Mulholland; Rides from Westside Los Angeles;
      San Fernando Valley to the Mountains; Topanga State Park
      MAPS: Dirt Mulholland/Topanga State Park   *26*
                  Will Rogers State Historic Park/Rogers Road Trail   *34*

3   **Topanga Canyon to**
      Las Virgenes/Malibu Canyon   *41*
      MAP: Old Topanga/Calabasas Peak/Stunt Road   *42*

4   **Las Virgenes/Malibu Canyon to Kanan-Dume**   *45*
      Malibu Creek State Park; Corral Canyon/Mesa Peak/
      Puerco Canyon; Solstice Canyon/Latigo Backbone Trail;
      Cheeseboro Canyon Park; Palo Comado/China Flats/
      Oak Park; Paramount Ranch
      MAPS: Malibu Creek State Park   *46*
                  Mesa Peak/Puerco Motorways   *54*
                  Solstice Canyon/Latigo/Zuma Canyon
                        Backbone Trail   *55*
                  Cheeseboro Canyon   *59*
                  Palo Comado Canyon/China Flat   *64*
                  Paramount Ranch   *70*

5   Kanan-Dume to Point Mugu   *73*
Zuma Canyon; Rocky Oaks National Recreation Area;
Charmlee Natural Area County Park; Circle X Ranch
MAPS: Zuma Ridge/Zuma Canyon   *72*
       Charmlee County Park   *78*
       Circle X Ranch   *80*

6   The Northern Santa Monicas   *83*
Westlake Open Space; Los Robles Canyon Open Space;
Wildwood Park; North Ranch Open Space; Point Mugu State Park;
Rancho Sierra Vista
MAPS: Westlake Open Space   *84*
       Los Robles Open Space   *89*
       Wildwood Park   *92*
       North Ranch Open Space   *97*
       Point Mugu State Park   *101*

7   Santa Susanna Mountains   *109*
Rocky Peak Park; Happy Camp Regional Park
MAPS: Rocky Peak Trail/Chumash Trail/
       Hummingbird Trail   *108*
       Happy Camp Regional Park   *114*

Appendices

IMBA Rules of the Trail   *120*
Fundamental Mountain Bike Skills   *121*
Access Points to the Santa Monicas   *126*
Agencies & Organizations with Programs
   in the Santa Monicas   *129*
Mountain Bike Equipment Checklist   *130*
First Aid   *132*
Selected References   *133*
Route Index   *134*
Outdoor Publications from Fine Edge Productions   *136*

Rogers Road Trail singletrack in Topanga State Park, north of Chicken Ridge.

Mark Langton

INTRODUCTION

Within minutes of Los Angeles, one of the largest urban centers in the country, the mountain bicyclist enters a more natural, more rugged world, and in striking contrast to the sprawling city and suburbs below. This is the Santa Monica Mountains National Recreation Area (SMMNRA), with more miles and more varied mountain bike riding than any other urban public backcountry area in the United States. Wildlife and natural vegetation abound; deer, bobcat and mountain lion are occasionally seen near residential developments.

From Griffith Park, in the center of Los Angeles, to Point Mugu State Park on the Pacific, the Santa Monicas stretch 52 miles in a northwesterly direction, providing a unique mixture of mountain, seashore and urban access to millions of visitors annually. But they unfold their treasures slowly: the more you go, the more you learn to appreciate the Santa Monica Mountains.

Until recently, the rugged terrain of these mountains was used only for ranching or recreation, but armed with new earth-moving equipment, developers began pushing their way into the mountains during the 1960s. At the petition of local environmentalists, Congress pledged to create the Santa Monica Mountains National Recreation Area in 1978.

But while the dream of a unified National Park in the Santa Monicas continues to this day, there still exists a virtual state of emergency for mountain park advocates. Developers continue filling in the canyons, and many tracts that might have been park land have been lost forever. Although over 60 agencies control lands in the Santa Monicas, undeveloped areas still need to be acquired and preserved for recreational use.

Perhaps the most significant acquisition in the short history of the SMMNRA took place in 1993, when cooperative efforts between Save Open Space, a citizen's action group, the Conservancy, and several dedicated politicians enabled the purchase of Palo Comado Canyon. This acquisition was beneficial in two ways; first, it stifled the efforts of developers who were planning an extensive community and golf course that would have threatened a major wildlife corridor and destroyed hundreds of native oak trees; and secondly, it effectively doubled the existing recreational park land acreage of Cheeseboro Canyon, making the combined park land the largest single public parcel in the SMMNRA.

Park supporters have renewed their efforts, and now they are joined by mountain bike activists. Save the Mountain Park Coalition achieved significant success when Congress appropriated $11 million for park land in 1988. President Bush, in his 1989 budget, indicated that urban parks like the Santa Monica Mountains National Recreation Area should be given the highest priority for federal support; however, budget cuts and an uncertain economy mean that the ultimate fate of the SMMNRA lies in the hands of the backcountry community to keep it alive and enjoyable for all who come. When visiting the SMMNRA, please consider it a privilege and an honor. There is no other place like it in the country.

TERRAIN

The Santa Monica Range is narrow—1 to 10 miles wide—and steep. Most canyons run in a north-south direction, carrying water either to the ocean or the inland valleys. Bicyclists usually find themselves climbing or descending; there is not much flat land or ridge riding. While this can be discouraging for beginners, some parks, such as Charmlee, Malibu Creek and Point Mugu, do offer great beginner rides. Once bicyclists are comfortable climbing long hills, they will be able to enjoy most of the rides in this Guide.

Most of the public land in the range is controlled by the National Park Service, California Department of Parks and Recreation, Los Angeles County, Ventura County, City of Thousand Oaks/Conejo Open Space Conservation Agency, Los Angeles City, Los Angeles County Sanitation District and the Los Angeles Department of Water and Power. The Santa Monica Mountains Conservancy is a state agency charged with the power to move swiftly and creatively in acquiring and using Santa Monica Mountains park lands.

A dry climate and good drainage makes for almost year-round riding in the Santa Monicas.

Brian Hemsworth

GEOLOGY

The Santa Monica Mountains—including the Channel Islands off the Ventura coast—were pushed up from the ocean floor some 10 million years ago. The careful observer will find fossils of ocean life throughout the range. Sedimentary rock makes up much of the mountains, and there are some stunning sandstone formations and shale walls. Some of the highest peaks, e.g., Castro Crest, Saddle Peak, Sandstone Peak and other mountains west of Malibu Canyon, show signs of volcanic activity dating back 20 million years or more.

FLORA

The Santa Monica range contains several plant communities, including grasslands, coastal sage and chaparral. While many visitors see only the "green season" and the "brown season," those familiar with the mountains will observe ever-changing foliage throughout the year. There are many species of wildflowers in the mountains; some varieties, such as the chocolate lily and the giant coreopsis, are found in very few locations around the world. The most prevalent flora is the chaparral system of dense, intermingled brush, which provides food and shelter to many small animals. The Santa Monicas are not heavily forested. Oaks dot the hillsides of north-facing slopes, huge sycamores are found along creek beds, and moister areas give rise to willows and cottonwoods. Poison oak abounds and, because its oil adheres to any surface, cyclists should be especially careful about laying their bikes down at the sides of the trail. Exotic (non-native) plants are plentiful. Wild mustard, thought to be native, was actually imported. Milk thistle, while beautiful in season, overruns the area and threatens several native species.

FAUNA

After years of human encroachment there are still some large animals in the Santa Monicas. Deer are plentiful in some of the parks. Bobcats abound, and cougars are still sighted in the rugged backcountry. Bears, once prevalent, were hunted to extinction, but there are now indications that bears are migrating from the Angeles Forest (to the north) as far as the Santa Susanna mountain corridor. This corridor, although it is now reduced to a single freeway underpass in undeveloped land, allows wildlife to cross into the Santa Monicas.

Many coyotes, raccoons, squirrels and other small mammals are seen, as are countless reptiles and birds. The mountains are home to several lizards and snakes, the Pacific rattlesnake being the most renown. Raptors—a few eagles and many varieties of hawks—fly the skies, and the raven and vulture are ubiquitous. Other birds include woodpeckers, hummingbirds and swallows. Point Mugu is a wintering site for Monarch butterflies that migrate from northern climates. Among the many varieties of insects in the Santa Monicas are some ferocious red ants.

Ticks and mosquitoes also present a danger that has recently caused concern. Lyme disease, carried by ticks, can cause prolonged illness and, in some cases, death. Ticks are most prevalent in spring, but are present year round. If you are riding in a brushy or grassy area and are coming into contact with a lot of branches, check frequently for ticks, especially under cuffs, waistbands, and socks. More recently, it has been discovered that a strain of encephalitis is carried by mosquitoes, especially in the Wildwood Park backcountry of the Conejo Open Space Conservation Agency (COSCA). Wear insect repellent if you are going to be riding near water where mosquitoes breed, such as Malibu Creek State Park, Rocky Oaks National Recreation Area, and Wildwood Park.

EARLY HISTORY

Located throughout the Santa Monicas are archaeological sites of the Chumash culture, Native Americans who inhabited coastal villages between present-day Los Angeles and San Luis Obispo. The Chumash were adept seafarers and astronomers known for their peaceful, culturally elaborate lifestyle. Displays and information about Chumash history are available at the Southwest Museum, the Malibu Creek State Park Information Center, the Malibu Lagoon Museum and at the Satwiwa Nature Center near the northern entrance to Point Mugu State Park at Rancho Sierra, a National Park Service site. The north side of the Santa Monicas was inhabited by two other tribal groups—Fernandeño and Gabrieleno Indians; like the Chumash, they were hunter-gatherers who thrived in the natural abundance of the range.

The Chumash are famous for their plank canoes and their basketry. While most other Native Americans of the period made dugout canoes or rafts, the Chumash were among the first people in the world to cut planks for constructing ocean-going vessels. The canoes were then sealed with beach tar from naturally occurring seeps. The tar was also used to seal water containers woven of yucca leaves or other plant material. Much in demand, these containers were traded widely; archaeologists have found them at sites hundreds of miles from the coast.

The Chumash are also known for their cave paintings, which depicted astronomical, hunting and historical symbols. One painting is executed so light falls on a particular symbol on the cave wall during the winter solstice. Another, showing riders on horseback, is believed to be the first native rendering of Europeans found in North America.

In 1769, the Portola expedition landed in Santa Monica Bay and began a long trek toward Monterey. Passing through the Santa Monica Mountains at what is now Sepulveda Pass on I-405, the Spaniards crossed the San Fernando Valley and continued toward Ventura. Father Crespi, the expedition's diarist, tells of descending the north slope of the Santa Monicas and seeing an enormous village at the site of today's Encino. The archaeological remains of the village have been discovered only recently, and some artifacts are currently on display at Los Encinos State Historical Park on Ventura Boulevard.

With Spanish colonization, the Chumash and other Southern California peoples were rounded up, merged, and renamed by the conquerors. The tribes, who had thrived on hunting, fishing and gathering, were forced into agriculture and Catholicism at Mission San Fernando and Mission Ventura. From the standpoint of anthropology and archaeology, much was lost when the Spanish destroyed the native lifestyle. Many Indians were thought to have escaped into the Santa Monicas, although the penalty, if they were caught, was extremely harsh. The missions were secularized between 1833 and 1840, and their extensive holdings were allocated to favored citizens. Many of the significant place names near the Santa

Monicas, including Tapia, Sepulveda and Verdugo, were the names of early land grant recipients. When Mexican forces surrendered to John C. Fremont at Cahuenga Pass in 1847, the Santa Monica Mountains were owned by a few, wealthy landholders. But over the years, the land was subdivided and parceled off to residents, investors, and public utility companies—a development pattern that still exists today.

RECREATIONAL ACCESS

Mulholland Highway runs the length of the Santa Monicas from Leo Carrillo State Beach near the Los Angeles-Ventura County Line to Hollywood's Cahuenga Pass. This road provides access to many of the best bicycling opportunities in the mountains. The 11-mile unpaved stretch between Encino Hills Drive and Topanga Canyon has limited traffic. It is not only rideable itself, but gives access to many fire roads on the west side of Los Angeles, San Fernando Valley and Topanga State Park. The Backbone Trail rises from Will Rogers State Historic Park off Sunset Boulevard and winds across the length of the mountains to Point Mugu State Park. When completed, this trail—comprised of both fire roads and singletrack—will allow cyclists to travel the east-west length of the mountains. While some sections are currently closed to bicycles, mountain bike activists are working to open the entire Backbone Trail to mountain bikes.

One of the greatest non-bicycling challenges for the mountain biker is learning where to park. Directions to fire roads and trails are rarely well marked, and word-of-mouth instructions are vague, at best. Residents in expensive neighborhoods adjacent to the Santa Monica Mountains don't always appreciate inquiries from backcountry users.

Here are some of the things you can do to promote access:

1. Never block fire road entrances or driveways.
2. Respect the rights and privacy of residents—don't make unnecessary noise and don't leave litter.
3. Be self-contained—don't ask for tools, water, a telephone or anything else unless it's an absolute emergency.
4. Always park legally.
5. If there's a self-registration day-use fee, pay it.

In the Appendix, you'll find "Access Points to the Santa Monicas," a parking guide for rides listed in this guide.

RIDE RESPONSIBLY!

Along with the miles of tremendous riding opportunities in the Santa Monicas come certain responsibilities and restrictions. Mountain bicyclists must be aware of current land management policies and honor all regulations; they must minimize impact on the land and be cognizant of the safety and enjoyment of other users. At press time, all the rides in this guide are legally open to bicyclists, but regulations are in flux and changes occur regularly. For up-to-date information contact the appropriate land managers.

A BRIEF HISTORY OF MOUNTAIN BIKING IN THE SANTA MONICAS

When chain-driven, small-wheeled "safety" bicycles first swept America around the turn of this century, they were inherently dirt bicycles, although not especially well suited for it. Most roads and trails were unpaved. Bicycles were primarily a means of transportation, and were used only secondarily for recreation. Los Angeles had a particularly active bicycling community in those days, and many bicycle pioneers who found their way to and through the Santa Monica Mountains were instrumental in getting roads and trails widened or graded and eventually paved. Then came the motorcar, and many of the bicycles that were used for transportation were abandoned for the internal combustion engine. Los Angeles has not, and may never, recover.

Bicyclists have long travelled the paved canyons of the Santa Monica Range. Seeing the connecting fire roads tempted many of them to try the dirt. They ventured into the mountains as far as they could go, carried their bikes when they had to, and did the necessary repairs when they got home. Many of these early mountain riders were road racers or bike shop employees. We know of riders who rode Rustic Canyon and the trails off Mulholland Drive as early as 1968-69. Like bicyclists everywhere, they tweaked their bikes to adapt to new conditions. They brazed cantilever brakes onto their road-racing or touring bikes and used sew ups while other road riders were still hiking. Meanwhile, kids from local neighborhoods discovered and rode the trails, ranch roads and service roads on their Sting Rays or paper boy bikes. People were biking in the mountains, but "mountain biking" was still waiting to happen.

Michael Hiltner was a 1960–64 Olympic road racer who set a double transcontinental record in 1975 by riding to the East Coast and back in 36 days, 8 hours. While on that ride, he changed his name to Victor Vincente of America because it captured his sense of bicycling excellence. When he began riding dirt roads around Dixie Canyon on his road bike in 1978, he could still return to a trail after several weeks and only see *his* tracks. According to Aaron Cox, Victor's riding buddy and a mountain bike racing pioneer, the discovery of someone else's tracks was cause for curiosity and excitement. Bike-to-bike encounters were rare, but the small Los Angeles mountain bike community was beginning to grow.

In 1979, two years after the mountain bike was "invented" in Marin County, Victor built his first "Topanga" mountain bike, a diamond frame with 20-inch wheels. He organized (in the loosest sense of the word) several of the first races and rides in the Santa Monicas. His early "Reseda to the Sea" races drew riders from all over the state, including mountain bike pioneer Gary Fisher, and the "Puerco Canyon" uphill/downhill races were proving grounds for many famous racers, including Ned Overend and John Tomac.

As mountain biking caught on, manufacturers began making multi-gear cruiser bikes with larger frames. Schwinn introduced its King Sting, and word about Northern California Fishers and Ritcheys was spreading. In 1980 there were regular downhill races in the nearby Verdugo and San Gabriel Mountains. And in early 1982, Specialized produced the Stumpjumper, the first mountain bike to be mass-marketed. The following year a dozen companies came out with "knock-offs," and a few bike shops introduced mountain bikes to the Los Angeles market. BMX racers, motorcyclists, and an assortment of hikers became mountain bikers themselves, and the number of mountain bicyclists in the Santa Monicas increased dramatically. Through bike shops and chance encounters on the trails, word spread about the network of byways that crossed the mountains. Access was easy and there was plenty of great riding.

By 1985, hundreds of mountain bicyclists were riding the Santa Monicas. Shops offered organized rides, and mountain biking was covered regularly by the bicycling press. That same year, Kevin Fox and Larry Shaw of the Hollywood YMCA founded the Adventure Trails Program to take inner city youths mountain biking in Sycamore Canyon. In this program, funded by the Santa Monica Mountains Conservancy and the Olympic Torch Fund, the kids learned about natural history and bicycle etiquette from the volunteer staff of local mountain bikers. Many kids were riding a derailleur bicycle for the first time, and the loop up Sycamore Canyon and back down Wood Canyon gave them a sense of personal accomplishment.

In 1985, opposition to backcountry bicycling developed as traditional user-groups voiced concern for personal safety and environmental damage. Many long-time environmentalists had lobbied hard to acquire park land, and a few had actually built the trails that bicyclists were using. Some had been startled or frightened by fast-moving bicyclists. Trails began to show wear from bicycle use and misuse. Remote areas which used to take hours to reach by foot or horse were being used regularly by bicyclists. The more traditional users felt that bicycles were moving onto their turf quickly and in large numbers. They pressured land managers to close the trails to cyclists.

In 1987, the Santa Monicas District State Parks closed most of Will Rogers State Historic Park to riding. They soon closed all singletrack trails in what was to become a precursor of the 1989 statewide policy. In August 1987, the Santa Monica Mountains Conservancy took up the issue of trail closures, and unlike earlier agency meetings, their hearing was announced ahead of time in the *Los Angeles Times*. Approximately 50 bicyclists attended, and although Conservancy officials did close the trails, they expressed willingness to work with organized groups of cyclists to re-open them. The cyclists had no organization to turn to, so on August 10, 1987, they met at the now defunct Santa Monica Mountain Bike Club to form CORBA, the Concerned Off-Road Bicyclists Association.

CORBA immediately began organizing area bicyclists. Many of the mountain bike pro shops offered financial and logistical support by sharing mailing lists and other resources. Dr. Al Farrell, a mountain bike enthusiast and benefactor of the National Off-Road Bicycle Association NORBA, supplied generous financial support. CORBA members began meeting with land managers and representatives of other user groups to convince them that mountain bicycles could be ridden safely and with minimal impact to the trails.

In 1988, the Angeles Chapter of the Sierra Club adopted a mountain bike policy proposed by member Tom Jeter which accepted the *possibility* of bicycles on trails. Previous policy had classified bicycles with motorcycles and dune buggies as just another "off-road vehicle." Representatives of CORBA, the Mount Wilson Bicycle Association and several Sierra Club bicyclists argued that the original policy was hostile and prejudicial, and they declared that bicyclists were legitimate backcountry users who had the same rights and responsibilities as hikers and equestrians.

As the mountain bike boom continues, land access has become a national issue. Groups are forming all over the nation to help educate the bicycling population and the public at large. The California Recreational Trails Council has recognized mountain biking as a viable backcountry recreation, and has worked with the mountain bike community to assess the access situation. IMBA, the International Mountain Bicycling Association, was founded by a coalition of local land access groups in California, including CORBA, Responsible Organized Mountain Peddlers (ROMP), The Bicycle Trails Council (BTC) of the East Bay, and BTC Marin. IMBA is an international umbrella organization that provides information to new mountain bike clubs, as well as working with federal organizations to establish mountain bike use policy. They also work closely with the bicycle industry and bicycle publications to ensure that the message of responsible riding is conveyed through advertising and editorial. The land access issue is perhaps the most overlooked yet important aspect of the bicycle industry; with the ongoing help of local clubs, bike shops, and the cycling press, mountain biking will continue to flourish.

In 1989, CORBA signed an agreement with the National Park Service and the California State Parks in the Santa Monicas to field a Volunteer Mountain Bike Unit (MBU) whose members are trained in first aid, CPR and interpretive skills. The MBU assists the ranger district in resource management and emergency situations, as well as helping all users with maps, water, and directions. They carry radios so they are in contact with emergency services and rangers, and have assisted in several emergency and evacuation procedures. In 1992, the MBU received one of the most prestigious awards in the bicycle industry, the Bicycle Federation of America's Pro Bike Award. Of 50 programs that were recognized, the MBU was the only mountain bike program. And in 1993, the MBU was honored by IMBA's Model Program Award, given each year to outstanding examples of mountain bike education and activism. On any given weekend or holiday you can see the brightly uniformed MBU patrolling in pairs on National and State Park lands. In fact, the MBU was the first mountain bike patrol of its kind to be cooperatively sponsored by both agencies. Recently the Conejo Open Space Conservation Agency (COSCA) launched its own multi-use patrol on its park lands using the model of the MBU. CORBA has also become active in trail-building and maintenance. The MBU's approximately 125-member patrol alone accounts for more volunteer hours annually than all other volunteer organizations *combined*.

The majority of the public singletrack trails in the Santa Monicas are closed to bicycles except on COSCA lands, which are completely multi-use except for a few trails that are too dangerous for bicycles and horses. COSCA property is used heavily by horseback riders and hikers, especially on weekends, so it is extremely important that you exercise utmost caution when riding on COSCA property. However, there are still many miles of singletrack trails open to mountain bikes in the Santa Monica Mountains, and typically they are popular among hikers and equestrians as well. Please use extreme caution whenever riding on narrow trails with limited lines of sight or when your sight line is decreased.

Please remember that the maximum speed limit for vehicles (including mountain bikes) is 15 miles per hour on all public backcountry roadways. Always control your speed and never go faster than the conditions safely allow. Radar guns are in use in some State Parks, such as Point Mugu, and cyclists are issued citations for exceeding the 15-mph speed limit. Check with CORBA or land managers for up-to-date information on mountain bike access.

All riders using this guide are part of the continuing history of cycling in these mountains. Be aware that mountain bike use is being monitored. *Ride responsibly.* Spread the word. Become involved with the groups that are trying to acquire and protect recreational land in the Santa Monicas.

In shady canyons or atop scenic ridges, you'll find that bicycling the Santa Monica Mountains offer more refuge and pleasure than you'd ever imagined. Yet the sound of earth movers is never far away. Once mountain backcountry is lost to recreation, it is lost forever. Mountain bicyclists have an important role in the preservation of the Santa Monica Mountains National Recreation Area. Please do your part to ensure a positive future for mountain biking!

Mark Langton

A rare Victor Vincente of America sighting! How can you tell this is a recent photo, even though the bike is the same he's been riding for over 15 years (same clothes, too)? Check out the clipless pedals! (Cheeseboro Canyon)

SPECIAL CONSIDERATIONS

by Don Douglass

This guide covers the Santa Monica Mountains from the Hollywood Hills to Point Mugu State Park, a region that includes remote areas and provides wide variations in climate, elevation, terrain, trail and road conditions. Good preparation will bring opportunities for pleasure; poor preparation invites disaster. To increase your pleasure in exploring the Santa Monicas by mountain bike we offer the following suggestions.

1. COURTESY. Know and follow the IMBA Rules of the Trail printed in the Appendix. Extend courtesy to all other trail users and follow the golden rule. Always ride as if to encounter another user around the next corner.

2. PREPARATIONS. Plan your trip carefully by developing a check list. Know your abilities and your equipment. Prepare to be self-sufficient at all times.

3. MOUNTAIN CONDITIONS. If you leave the coastline, be prepared for:

• *Sun:* Protect your skin against the sun's harmful rays. The higher you go, the more damaging the sun becomes. Use sunscreen with a rating of 15 or more. Wear a light-colored long-sleeved shirt or jersey, and a hat with a wide brim. Guard against heatstroke in these desert-like mountains by riding in early morning or late afternoon when the sun's rays are less intense.

• *Low Humidity:* Start each trip with a minimum of two or more full water bottles or one full "camelbak." Generally, water is not available in the Santa Monicas. *Gallons* of water may not be sufficient for *really* hot weather. Force yourself to drink, whether or not you feel thirsty. Untreated drinking water may cause Giardiasis or other diseases. Carry water from a known source, or treat it.

• *Variations in Temperature and Weather Conditions:* You may find it cool and foggy on the coastal side of a ridge, and hot and dry on the other. Carry extra clothing—a windbreaker, gloves, stocking cap—and use the multi-layer system so you can adjust according to conditions. Keep an eye on changing cloud and wind conditions. Wind, as well as changes in weather, can deplete your energy.

• *Fatigue:* Sluggish or cramping muscles and fatigue indicate the need for calories. Carry high-energy snack foods such as granola bars, dried fruits and nuts to maintain strength and warmth, and add clothing layers as the temperature drops or the wind increases.

• *Know how to deal with dehydration, hypothermia, altitude sickness, sunburn or heatstroke.* Be sensitive at all times to the natural environment: the land can be frightening and unforgiving. If you break down, it may take you longer to walk out than it took you to ride in! Check with your local Red Cross, Sierra Club, or mountaineering textbooks for detailed information.

4. NAVIGATION. Use all available topographic and USFS maps. *There are numerous errors in the published data of the Coast Range, particularly the older 15-minute USGS topo maps, so you need to check and make comparisons between maps.* Use the new 7.5 series quadrangle topo maps as they become available and the Fine Edge Production mountain biking topographical map. *The maps in this volume are designed as an aid only, to help you find the right starting points or to interpret official maps.*

Before you leave on your trip, tell someone where you're going, when you expect to return, and what to do in case you don't return on time. Ask them to call the Los Angeles County Sheriff or the Park Ranger if you are more than six hours overdue, giving full details about your vehicle and trip plans.

It's easy to get lost. Have a plan ready in advance with your group in case you lose your way. En route, keep track of your position on your trip map(s); record the times you arrive at known places on the map. Be sure to look back frequently in the direction from which you came, in case you need to retrace your path. Do not be afraid to turn back when conditions change, or the going is rougher than you expected.

If you have arranged to meet someone, allow enough time. It frequently takes both parties longer to rendezvous than expected. Meet at a road intersection that cannot be confused by either party. (It's difficult to locate someone in a large campground!) Write down instructions for both parties before you leave.

At times it may be difficult to determine which roads and trails are open to public travel. When in doubt, make local inquiries. Follow signs and leave all gates either opened or closed, as you found them, or as signed. Park off the road, even in remote areas, so you do not block emergency vehicles.

5. HORSES. Many of the trails in the Santa Monicas are used by recreational horse riders. Some horses are spooked easily, so make them aware of your presence *well in advance of the encounter.* A startled horse can cause serious injuries both to the rider and to itself.

If you come upon horses moving *toward* you, yield the right-of-way, even when it seems inconvenient. Carry your bike to the downhill side and stand quietly, well off the trail in a spot where the animals can see you clearly. Talk to the rider and horse so that the horse recognizes the bike as something "human," which will calm it and make it less likely to spook when it sees a bike and rider on the trail the next time.

If you come upon horses *moving ahead of you in the same direction,* stop well behind them. Do not attempt to pass until you have alerted the riders and asked for permission. Then, pass on the downhill side of the trail or as instructed by the rider, talking to the horse and rider as you do.

It is your responsibility to ensure that such encounters are safe for everyone.

6. RESPECT THE ENVIRONMENT. Minimize your impact on the natural environment. *Remember, mountain bikes are not allowed in Wilderness Areas and in certain other restricted areas.* Ask, when in doubt; you are a visitor. Leave plants and animals alone; historic and cultural sites untouched. Stay on established roads and trails, and do not enter private property. Follow posted instructions and use good common sense. Don't be a "backcountry pioneer" who

strays from established trails, spoiling untouched terrain, and ruining the name of mountain biking for other responsible mountain cyclists.

7. CONTROL AND SAFETY. Control your mountain bike at all times. Guard against excessive speed. Avoid overheated rims and brakes on long or steep downhill rides. Lower your center of gravity by lowering your seat on downhills. Lower your tire pressure on rough or sandy stretches. Use appropriate safety equipment, such as helmet, gloves, protective clothings, etc. Carry first aid supplies and bike tools for emergencies. *Avoid solo travel in remote areas.*

SUPPORT MOUNTAIN BIKE LAND ACCESS!

These volunteer non-profit organizations need your help:

Concerned Off-Road Bicyclists Association
P.O. Box 784, Woodland Hills, CA 91365-0784
Phone: (818) 773-3555 • www.corbamtb.com

International Mountain Bicycling Association
P.O. Box 7578, Boulder, CO 80306-7578
Phone: (303) 545-9011 • Fax: (303) 545-902 • www.imba.com

CHAPTER 1

The Eastern Santa Monicas

Griffith Park; Lake Hollywood Reservoir;
Cross Mountain Park—TreePeople, Franklin
Canyon and Wilacre Park

The Eastern Santa Monica Mountains begin at Griffith Park and extend to Sepulveda Pass at I-405 (San Diego Freeway). This area of the mountains has been heavily developed and as a result has very little legal riding. Those areas that are legal are frequently congested with bicyclists, hikers, picnickers and equestrians. Griffith Park and Lake Hollywood Reservoir offer some nice rides for beginners just getting used to their bikes, for riders with kids, or for anyone who wants to toodle around on nice days. The Cross Mountain Park areas (Franklin Canyon, TreePeople and Wilacre Park) enable more-experienced riders to connect trails and fire roads for rides of up to 20 miles in length. The riding in this area is not only diverse, but it combines relatively undeveloped backcountry riding with trails adjacent to main thoroughfares and million-dollar homes.

GRIFFITH PARK

Access: Travel Town parking lot is off 134 Freeway and Forest Lawn Boulevard at the northwest corner of the park. There's additional parking at the Greek Theatre on Vermont Avenue, on Fern Dell Canyon off Western Avenue, and at several other small sites.

A few years ago, Griffith Park closed all of its dirt roads and trails to bicycles because of complaints by equestrians. This is a very crowded multiple-use area. The many paved roads within the park are open to bicycles, however, and offer interesting, scenic loops. Most roads are closed to auto traffic on weekends, so there are many smooth places to ride. Some of the favorite bicycle rides begin at Travel Town on the northwest side of the park. From here you can ride through the park, up to the observatory, around the golf courses, or over to the zoo.

Lake Hollywood Reservoir

Mileage: 3.5 mile loop.
Level of Difficulty: Easy.
Access: From the west on Barham Street, take Lake Hollywood Drive past Wonderview, then descend and park by the chain link fence on the right. You'll see old motorcycle trails climbing hills to the left.

Lake Hollywood Reservoir was built by William Mulholland, the architect and water engineer responsible for many of the dams and aqueducts that supply Los Angeles with water. The reservoir earned its greatest notoriety when it collapsed in the movie *Earthquake* and flooded the city of Hollywood to the south. The area is open from 6:30 to 10:00 a.m. and 2:00 to 6:00 p.m. weekdays and from 6:30 a.m. to 6:00 p.m. on weekends.

This 3.5-mile loop around the lake on a blacktop service road is a nice, flat beginner ride that's especially well suited for riding with children. The lake itself is fenced off from the bike path preventing use of the water or shoreline. One mile from the northwest gate you'll cross the dam to an area well shaded by pine and eucalyptus. From here you

have great views of Hollywood to the south and the Hollywood Hills to the north and east. You'll see the Hollywood sign on Mount Lee, probably one of the most famous landmarks in Los Angeles. It was built in 1923 to

Mark Langton in his glory days.

Steve Giberson

advertise the "Hollywoodland" real estate development in Beachwood Canyon below. Over the years, letters fell down and the sign was frequently vandalized. It was restored in the 1970s to read *Hollywood* in fifty-foot letters.

On weekends, this area can be very crowded. North of the lake, the closed gate leads to an area of several old motorcycle trails and short, dead-end access roads to electric towers. These are rideable, but not very exciting.

CROSS MOUNTAIN PARK
TreePeople/Franklin Canyon/Wilacre Park

Access: TreePeople Headquarters at the junction of Coldwater Canyon, Franklin Canyon and Mulholland Drive. From the east it's 2.9 miles from Laurel Canyon and Mulholland Drive; from the west, it's 5.2 miles from I-405.

TreePeople, Franklin Canyon and Wilacre Park together comprise Cross Mountain Park. The TreePeople manage a park at the junction of Mulholland and Coldwater canyons, and it is a convenient place to park for rides south into Franklin Canyon and north to Wilacre Park. It's shady, with plenty of parking, water, bathrooms and several picnic areas. The buildings here were from an old fire station that dates back to 1923.

The TreePeople advocate the Urban Forest principle, a philosophy extolling the planting of trees in urban areas as a source of shade, food, clean air, and aesthetic pleasure. They plant several thousand trees a year in Los Angeles, maintain a nursery and reference library, and provide educational programs for both children and adults. The fire roads north of TreePeople lead to Wilacre Park and Fryman Canyon. The north and south loops make a challenging and diverse 20-mile loop.

TreePeople to Franklin Canyon

Mileage: 3.8 miles one way.
Level of Difficulty: Easy.

0.0 mile: TreePeople parking lot. Turn left (east) on Mulholland Drive. At 0.3 mile there is a junction with Coldwater Canyon (south). 0.9 mile: Turn right on the dirt road marked *Private road, Guard dogs on duty.* At mile 1.0 go through the fire gate onto the dirt road and begin a gradual climb. At 1.6 and 1.9 miles, two singletracks drop down steeply into Franklin Canyon. Stay on the main road; do not take the singletracks. Descent begins at 1.9 mile. At 2.3 you pass a sign on the left—*Hastain Trail, No Bikes*—and continue descending to the fire gate at 3.3 miles and a junction with a paved road. A right turn goes up out of the canyon and back to TreePeople. The left leads to a dead end at 3.8 miles. There are restrooms, water, a picnic area and a ranger station on the south side of the park.

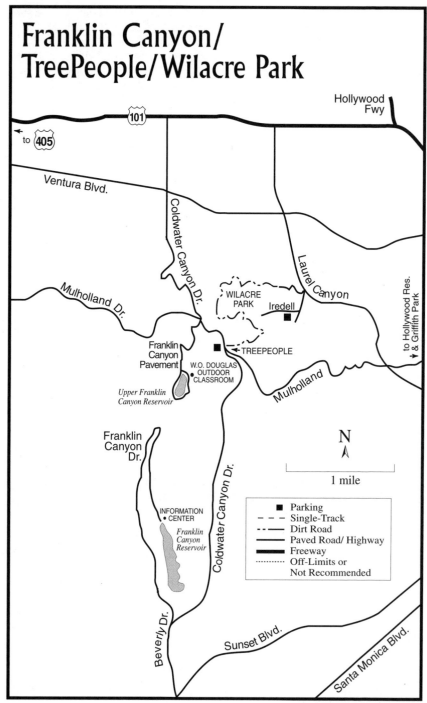

Franklin Canyon/ TreePeople/Wilacre Park

Hollywood Fwy

101

to 405

Ventura Blvd.

Coldwater Canyon Dr.

Mulholland Dr.

Laurel Canyon

to Hollywood Res. & Griffith Park

WILACRE PARK

Iredell

Franklin Canyon Pavement

W.O. DOUGLAS OUTDOOR CLASSROOM

← TREEPEOPLE

Mulholland

Upper Franklin Canyon Reservoir

Franklin Canyon Dr.

N

1 mile

■ Parking
– – – Single-Track
–·–·– Dirt Road
——— Paved Road/ Highway
━━━ Freeway
·········· Off-Limits or Not Recommended

INFORMATION
• CENTER

Franklin Canyon Reservoir

Coldwater Canyon Dr.

Beverly Dr.

Sunset Blvd.

Santa Monica Blvd.

© 1998 Fine Edge Productions

Franklin Canyon Pavement Climb

Mileage: 2 miles one way.
Level of Difficulty: Easy.

The climb out of Franklin Canyon begins on the paved road by the ranger station and climbs 2 miles to Mulholland Drive and TreePeople. Sometimes an alternative loop is open on the right, that takes you past the reservoir and the new William O. Douglas classroom before connecting back to the main road.

Picnic Overlook in TreePeople

Mileage: 1 mile.
Level of Difficulty: Easy.

In the northeast corner of the TreePeople property (by the nursery) there is a short half-mile out-and-back ride to a spectacular picnic area overlooking San Fernando Valley. The bark-covered road passes through a shady eucalyptus grove to the overlook. There is a sign asking bikes to observe a 5 m.p.h. speed limit since many families and hikers use this area.

Magic Forest Trail

Mileage: Loops of 3 to 4 miles.
Level of Difficulty: Easy.

Magic Forest Trail is the main descent out of TreePeople. There are several marked sites where particular vegetation or animal habitats can be observed. The trailhead is on the northwest side of the parking area.

0.0 mile: Begin the Magic Forest Trail. Within a short distance, you have the choice of descending alongside some steps, or leaving the park through the fire gate and reentering it in a few yards through another fire gate. In either case, you'll descend 0.3 mile to a junction with another fire road and a sign that indicates this is Santa Monica Mountains Conservancy property. Here you begin a loop through Fryman Canyon.

Turning left (west) you have a gradual climb up a fire road that peaks before dropping down to Fryman Canyon and Wilacre Park. Toward the bottom the road is paved. A more challenging route begins at 0.48 mile, where a steep singletrack cuts off to the right. This puts you in "Baja" (BMX heaven in earlier days) where the canyon is crisscrossed by several singletrack trails, all of which empty out approximately 1.5 miles down the fire road in Fryman Canyon. Wilacre Park, managed by the Santa Monica Mountains Conservancy, has shaded areas and picnic tables. The singletrack trails are closed to bikes.

Exit Wilacre Park at Fryman Road, turn right on Iredell Street, then left on Iredell Lane. This takes you to a cul-de-sac and a fire gate entrance that leads 0.5 mile back to TreePeople junction.

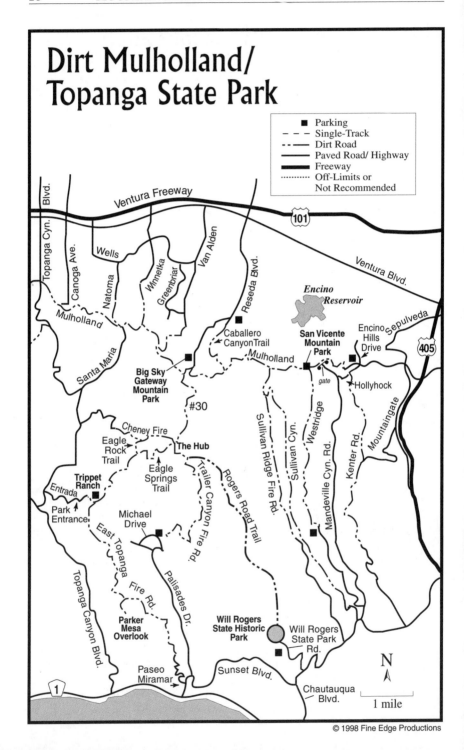

Dirt Mulholland/ Topanga State Park

Legend:
- ■ Parking
- – – – Single-Track
- –·–·– Dirt Road
- ——— Paved Road/ Highway
- ▬▬▬ Freeway
- ·········· Off-Limits or Not Recommended

CHAPTER 2

Sepulveda Pass to Topanga Canyon

East Side Dirt Mulholland; Rides from Westside Los Angeles; San Fernando Valley to the Mountains; Topanga State Park

This is probably the area most widely ridden by westside Los Angeles and San Fernando Valley bicyclists. There are many access points on both sides of the mountains. A large number of fire roads provide opportunities for loop trips. Within a few minutes of entering the mountains, you may encounter deer, coyote, bobcat, hawks and other wildlife. The peaks and rock formations of Topanga State Park offer stunning views. Trails climb from the cool, shady canyon bottomland to the ridges of Dirt Mulholland. You can create rides of any length by making connections between the many fire roads in the area. Here, too, you'll see the imminent threat of development. Canyons have been filled, peaks graded, and oaks felled as Pacific Palisades and the San Fernando Valley continue to sprawl.

EAST SIDE DIRT MULHOLLAND

Access: Dirt Mulholland and Encino Hills Road. From the east take I-405, exit at Mulholland, follow the signs to Mulholland Drive, and turn left (west). Go 2.1 miles to the fork with Encino Hills Drive. Turn left onto dirt and go 0.2 mile to a parking area by a concrete blockhouse. From the north take Havenhurst south across Ventura Boulevard into the hills. The second stop sign is at a T; bear right on Havenhurst (left is Lanai), and continue past stop signs at Bosque, Adlon and Escalon. Turn right at the stop sign at Encino Hills Drive. Follow Encino Hills Drive up and around, past houses and an exposed dirt hill, to the fork. Bear right to Dirt Mulholland (left is paved Mulholland) and park by the concrete blockhouse.

Rogers Road Trail in Topanga State Park, just north of Will Rogers State Historic Park. Above are Chicken Ridge and Gobbler's Knob overlook.

Dirt Mulholland is rutted and bumpy with the risk of off-highway vehicles and tourists' rental cars around every corner. Most bicycle riding is done on the fire roads that connect Dirt Mulholland to the San Fernando Valley and the west side of Los Angeles. The following list (east to west) shows distances between the fire roads off Dirt Mulholland. Mileages are from the concrete blockhouse at Dirt Mulholland and Encino Hills Drive, and the direction each road leads off Mulholland is given in parentheses:

0.0	Park	Mountaingate/Mandeville Canyon/Kenter fire road (beginning of Dirt Mulholland)
0.75	(S)	Westridge fire road/San Vicente Mountain Park (turn-out parking)
1.71	(S)	Sullivan OTH fire road and gate
1.95	(N)	#27 Zelzah fire road
2.05	(S)	Farmer Ridge fire road
3.39	(N)	#28 Reseda-Caballero Canyon
4.80	(S)	#30 fire road
6.30	(N)	Van Alden
6.70	(N)	Gleneagles
7.13	(N)	Winnetka
7.74	(N)	Natoma
7.74	(S)	Santa Maria
8.24	(N)	Canoga

Mountaingate/Mandeville Canyon (Kenter) Fire Road

Mileage: 1.55 miles one way.
Level of Difficulty: Easy.

At 0.0 mile, go through the fire gate to the left of the blockhouse. Go straight just past mile 1 (there is a possible right at the rock pile on Hollyhock that descends to Mandeville Canyon, a ride that is described below). At mile 1.2 go straight through an open gate. At 1.5 miles there is a closed gate turn-around at Mountaingate. On the other side of the fence is Canyonback Road, and the Kenter fire road resumes a half-mile south. If you wish, carry your bike around the fence, ride south on Canyonback, and enter the fire road at the white gate (see Kenter Fire Road below).

Hollyhock to Mandeville Canyon

Mileage: 1.1 miles one way.
Level of Difficulty: Easy.

When descending the Mountaingate fire road from Dirt Mulholland, you will see a large pile of rocks on the right of the trail at 1.1 miles. This marks the Hollyhock descent to Mandeville Canyon, which allows you to loop over to the Westridge fire road (see below). Go right at the rock pile onto this old, bumpy, blacktop descent. Looking west, you'll see roads climbing up from the west side of Mandeville Canyon, roads you will take momentarily. After a 0.8-mile drop, the trail exits through a sycamore grove. Go through a locked gate very near private property (street sign: *3700 North Hollyhock Place*). If you were thinking of starting a ride here, be advised that there is *no legal parking.*

Turn right (north). At 0.3 mile turn left on Gardenland Road. Westridge fire road climbs left from the cul-de-sac (parking may be available).

Gardenland to Westridge

Mileage: 1.4 miles one way.
Level of Difficulty: Moderate climb.

0.0 mile: Begin fire road. At 0.5 mile there is a fork in the road. Climb right toward an electric tower. (The left descends steeply 0.7 mile to a dead end at another tower.) At mile 0.9 the road joins Westridge fire road at a chain link fence a half-mile south of the Nike Base.

Zelzah Fire Road

Mileage: 0.8 mile out-and-back.
Level of Difficulty: Easy.

Zelzah fire road (#27) is located just short of 2 miles west of the concrete blockhouse at the beginning of Dirt Mulholland, and it drops 0.4 mile on a steep, sandy road north to an impassable gate near Lake Encino. There's no way out, so you must climb back up.

RIDES FROM WESTSIDE LOS ANGELES

Kenter Fire Road

Access: Turn right on Kenter from Sunset Boulevard 1.1 miles west of 405 Freeway. Follow Kenter 2.3 miles up a gradually steeper hill to a parking area by a yellow fire gate.

This fire road used to go all the way to the east side of Dirt Mulholland, coming out by the concrete blockhouse near Encino Hills Drive. Now it is cut off by the Mountaingate development. You can still ride the entire length of the dirt road by lifting your bike over the gate on the south side of Mountaingate, riding a short distance on Canyonback Road, and finding a way around the fence on the north side of Mountaingate. This ride description deals only

Rogers Road Trail singletrack in Topanga State Park, north of Chicken Ridge.

Mark Langton

with the ride from the Kenter fire gate to Mountaingate. (See Mountaingate-Mandeville-Kenter Fire Road and Hollyhock to Mandeville above for a description of the ride from Mulholland.)

0.0 mile: Enter Kenter fire road at the yellow gate. There is an immediate, steep 0.1-mile climb that crests and goes into a short downhill. All along Kenter there are dead-end side roads to electric towers. Stay on the main road; it is wide and well-graded. Mandeville Canyon is below to the west, and you can see the Gardenland Road climbing to Westridge on the other side of the canyon. Just past 1.5 miles go through an open gate signed Mountain District. Immediately this passes through a fence and climbs to a green storage tank just short of mile 2.

Pavement begins at 2.0 miles, and at about 2.4 the road drops steeply to a white gate in the Mountaingate community. Either return down Kenter or, if you go through the gate and turn left on paved Canyonback Road, follow the ridge for about a half-mile to a chain link fence by some tennis courts. The Mountaingate fire road to Dirt Mulholland is on the other side of the fence to the left.

Westridge Fire Road

Mileage: 3.6 miles one way.
Level of Difficulty: Moderate climb.
Access: Exit I-405 at Sunset Boulevard and head west 2.3 miles to Mandeville Canyon. Turn right and continue 0.3 mile to Westridge, where you turn left. Climb 2.3 miles to a dead end at a fire gate. Please obey all parking signs.

This is a moderate climb connecting Dirt Mulholland to Westridge. By combining Westridge, Sullivan Ridge, Sullivan Canyon and Dirt Mulholland, you can easily make several loops. The road climbs from Westridge Road along a ridge that overlooks Sullivan and Rustic canyons.

Rogers Road Trail in Topanga State Park, just north of Will Rogers State Historic Park.

Mark Langton

Many people return to Westridge Road via the singletrack along the ridge above the fire road. There are several points along the fire road that allow access to the trail. Use caution as there are several steep and rutted sections.

0.0 mile: Moderate climb. 1.0 mile: Flat overlook. 2.0 mile: Flat overlook. To the left at mile 3.5 a dead-end electric tower service road comes in. Go straight. At mile 3.6 go through a gate to San Vicente Mountain Park and Dirt Mulholland. SVMP is a great place to rest and enjoy the view of Los Angeles. There are restrooms, water, and picnic tables.

Sullivan Canyon Trail

Mileage: 4.5 miles one way.
Level of Difficulty: Moderate; some steep climbs.
Access: Turn right off Sunset Boulevard at Mandeville Canyon. At 0.3 mile turn left onto Westridge, then left again on Bayliss. Turn left on Queensferry and park along Queensferry or on Bayliss.

Sullivan Canyon Trail connects Dirt Mulholland to Queensferry. This is one of the coolest, prettiest rides on the eastern side of the Santa Monicas. It follows a creek bed up the canyon where, on the north side, it climbs steeply up to the Sullivan fire road.

0.0 mile: Trail entrance at a wooden gate at Queensferry. Descend the steep paved section 0.25 mile to the bottom and turn right. At 3.5 miles you begin to climb steeply. At mile 4.0 the trail ends at a T in a concrete basin. The right climbs a half-mile and dead-ends; the left climbs a half-mile to Sullivan Ridge fire road. Turn right to Mulholland.

Sullivan Ridge Fire Road

Mileage: 3.7 miles one way.
Level of Difficulty: Generally moderate. The singletrack parallel route requires expert climbing abilities.
Access: From I-405, west 4 miles along Sunset, right onto Amalfi and follow to a Y. Bear left. At the stop sign, turn left on Capri. Follow it to a T intersection, then go left on Casale to a turnout parking area. Take the paved road 2.5 miles to the gate at the fire road and Camp Josepho Boy Scout Camp. Sullivan Ridge fire road connects Dirt Mulholland and Amalfi Drive.

0.0 mile: Enter the fire road through the gate. At about 2.8 miles a fire road on the right comes up from Sullivan Canyon. Continue straight. At mile 3.7 is a fire gate at Dirt Mulholland (about 1 mile west of Westridge fire road). A singletrack parallels the fire road most of the way. It's pretty steep in places. There are plenty of connectors back to the fire road between Mulholland and the fire gate.

Descending Rogers Road Trail in Topanga State Parks at Gobbler's Knob overlook.

Mark Langton

Will Rogers State Historic Park/ Rogers Road Trail (Backbone Trail)

Mileage: 6.5 miles one way.
Level of Difficulty: Moderate to very difficult with very steep climbs, very technical singletrack.
Access: From I-405, go west 5.5 miles to Will Rogers State Park Road, turn right to main parking lot at top of hill. From main lot, take access road to the right of the large lawn in front of house.

Will Rogers State Historic Park is located on the 186-acre ranch site of actor and philosopher Will Rogers. Donated to the State Parks in 1944 after the death of Rogers' wife, Betty, it is extremely popular because of the beautiful grounds and self-guided tours of the 31-room ranch house, maintained as it was when Rogers and his family lived there from 1928-1935. The park is a major link into Topanga State Park to the north. It also serves as a major staging area for equestrians. Please use extra caution when using the trails emanating from this area.

Rogers Road Trail (Backbone Trail) is the major access trail into the Santa Monica Mountains from western Los Angeles and cities south, such as Marina Del Rey, Palos Verdes, Redondo Beach, and Long Beach. It is extremely popular with hikers and equestrians, as well as visitors not experienced with the mountains. The trail offers a spectacular view of Downtown and West Los Angeles, as well as the Santa Monica Bay, Palos Verdes Peninsula, and Catalina Island. Because of this the trail is very busy on weekends with all types of users. It is very narrow and technical in places, so control your speed whenever descending Rogers Road Trail, and especially the one-mile section between Inspiration Point

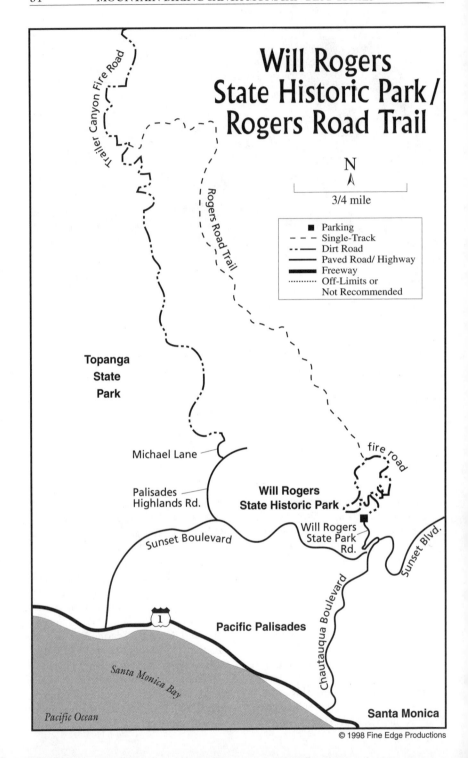

Will Rogers State Historic Park / Rogers Road Trail

N
∧

3/4 mile

- ■ Parking
- – – Single-Track
- –·–· Dirt Road
- —— Paved Road/ Highway
- ▬▬ Freeway
- ········· Off-Limits or Not Recommended

Trailer Canyon Fire Road

Rogers Road Trail

Topanga State Park

fire road

Michael Lane

Palisades Highlands Rd.

Will Rogers State Historic Park

Will Rogers State Park Rd.

Sunset Boulevard

Sunset Blvd.

Chautauqua Boulevard

Pacific Palisades

Santa Monica Bay

Pacific Ocean

Santa Monica

© 1998 Fine Edge Productions

Loop Trail in the State Historic Park and Gobbler's Knob.

Will Rogers State Historic Park has a loop trail that connects to the base of Rogers Road Trail. It is a two-mile loop that is wide fire road and leads in either direction from the Ranch House to Inspiration Point. No other trails in the State Historic Park are open to bikes.

From the parking lot, ride up the paved access road to the right of the large lawn in front of the Ranch House, marked *Authorized Vehicles Only*. Ride just past 0.1 to a T, with stables and a training corral directly in front of you. Either left or right will take you to Rogers Road Trail. Stay on designated trails only. Both directions offer interesting views of the ocean and surrounding neighborhoods of Brentwood and Pacific Palisades. While both are almost identical in length, the right (east) direction is a bit more interesting: Follow the paved road between the small ranch house and storage sheds, onto the dirt road. At 0.5 there is a Y; stay right and continue to mile 1.0 (0.9 if you take the left route) to the entrance to Rogers Road Trail and boundary of Topanga State Park, marked by an informational kiosk and multi-use sign. The trail begins climbing steeply and has several large railroad ties. Just past mile 1.7 you come to Chicken Ridge and a bridge. Please heed the "walk your bikes" section, approximately 100 yards ("shut up and walk!") to the knob above, known as Gobbler's Knob.

Once at Gobbler's Knob, remount and continue on Rogers Road Trail. At mile 2.0 a trail comes in from

Rogers Road Trail singletrack in Topanga State Park, north of Chicken Ridge.

Mark Langton

the right. At the time of this printing the trail was closed to bikes. However, this trail leads down to Rustic Canyon and Camp Josepho Boy Scout Camp, creating a connector to Sullivan Ridge. It is very poorly built and is barely walkable, let alone rideable.

Continuing on Rogers Road Trail, At 3.2 miles you come to an overlook turnout with a four-trunked oak tree ("Lone Oak Overlook"). To the east are two ridges; the closer ridge is Sullivan, while the farther is Westridge.

Turning west and continuing, the trail levels out into a very overgrown section known as the Jungle. It contains large amounts of poison oak on either side of the trail, so use caution. At 6.5 miles the trail meets Trailer Canyon Fire Road (Fire Road #30), approximately a half mile south of Hub Junction.

Trailer Canyon

Mileage: 4.5 miles one way.
Level of Difficulty: Moderate to difficult climb.
Access: On Sunset Boulevard, 7.9 miles west of I-405, turn right on Palisades Drive. Go 2.5 miles and turn left at Vereda de la Montura. Then make a quick right at Michael Drive. Go 0.5 mile to entrance on left.

This ride has a steep uphill to the Hub in Topanga State Park, which is better ridden downhill. (See Temescal/Trailer Canyon below.) 0.0 mile: Entrance off Michael Drive. At mile 0.9 there is a closed fire gate. Mile 2.3 marks the junction with Temescal Canyon on the right (fire road for about 0.5 mile, then singletrack, currently closed to bikes). Bear left. At 2.4 miles there is an open fire gate, and at mile 4.5 you reach the Hub.

Paseo Miramar

Mileage: 6 miles.
Level of Difficulty: Difficult climb.
Access: From I-405 head west on Sunset Boulevard 8 miles to Paseo Miramar, just before PCH. Turn right and follow the yellow lines 1.3 miles uphill to a dead end at the fire gate.

This very steep, relentless climb rises from the fire gate at Paseo Miramar past the Hub to Trippet Ranch in Topanga State Park. At 2.2 miles you come to the junction with Parker Mesa Overlook. If you turn left and ride a half-mile, you'll have a great view of Santa Monica Bay. If you turn right, you'll climb (with some descents) to Trippet Ranch and Topanga State Park.

SAN FERNANDO VALLEY TO THE MOUNTAINS

Reseda to the Hub

Mileage: Options of 10 to 30 miles.
Level of Difficulty: Moderate to difficult.
Access: From San Fernando Valley exit Hwy. 101 at Reseda Boulevard and go south into the Santa Monica Mountains. Reseda used to end at a locked gate 2 miles south of Freeway 101 at the entrance to Brae Mar Country Club. Recent construction has extended it all the way up to 1/4 mile below Mulholland Drive. You may either park along the road near the Brae Mar entrance and access Caballero Canyon via the trail off the side of the road (south), or continue up Reseda 1.3 miles and park at Marvin Braude Gateway Park. Starting at Mulholland will eliminate the Caballero Canyon Climb (also known as Dirt Reseda or Reseda fire road) and about a half-mile of Mulholland on the way to Fire Road #30 and Topanga State Park.

"Reseda to the Sea" was a race and then a ride sponsored by Victor Vincente, the Santa Monica Mountains bicycle pioneer. The ride typically climbed to the Hub in Topanga State Park, descended to Pacific Palisades on Trailer Canyon fire road, climbed back up Paseo Miramar to Trippet Ranch and Eagle Rock and then returned to the Hub and Reseda fire road. Less ambitious riders have a number of options. *Caution: The Reseda fire road is often congested.*

0.0 mile: Parking area at Brae Mar. The trail climbs gradually to 0.8 miles, then gets very steep as it makes a hairpin turn around a sycamore tree. It's 1.5 miles to Dirt Mulholland. Look to the north for a great view of San Fernando Valley. Across the road on the south side of Mulholland is the trailhead to Middle Bent Arrow singletrack, which is currently *closed to bikes.* Turn right on Mulholland. Close to mile 1.9 is Lower Bent Arrow singletrack, which is also closed. At 2.3 miles the access to Marvin Braude Gateway Park comes in from the right (north). Climb about 2.8 to fire road #30, the entrance to Topanga State Park, on the left.

At 4.9 miles, you reach the Hub where four roads cross: #30; Eagle Rock Road to the north; Eagle

Rogers Road Trail singletrack in Topanga State Park, north of Chicken Ridge. There's plenty of room for all users!

Mark Langton

Springs Road, middle right; and Temescal Canyon to Will Rogers/ Temescal/Trailer canyons to the south (see below). The sign reads: *1.9 to Mulholland Temescal Ridge Trail, 0.7 to Eagle Rock North Loop Trail, 1.0 to Eagle Springs Backbone Trail, 0.5 to Rogers Road, 4.8 Temescal Ridge to Conference Grounds.*

Eagle Rock/Eagle Springs Loop

Mileage: 2-mile loop.
Level of Difficulty: Moderate.

Follow the route description for Reseda to the Hub (above) to mile 4.9. Take Eagle Rock Road (on the north) to a good overlook at about 5.5 miles. On a clear day you have

views of Calabasas, Topanga, Eagle Rock, the East Topanga fire road, the Eagle Springs fire road, the red roofs of Santa Ynez Canyon houses, the Palisades, Catalina Island (if you're lucky), Cathedral Rock and the Hub. Eagle Rock Road is a steep downhill, sandy and chopped up. Look out for climbing hikers, horses and bicycles. At mile 5.8 continue straight at the fork with Cheney fire road on the right. (Cheney fire road is a rough descent to paved Cheney Drive, which drops down to Topanga Canyon Boulevard.)

Mile 6, Eagle Rock, on the left is a sandstone outcropping from which you have some stunning views of the mountains and the ocean. It has a 2,105-foot elevation and drops off sharply on the south side to the Eagle Springs Road below. There are caves on the south side of the rock as well. From here, you can see East Topanga fire road, which descends to Trippet Ranch, as well as Eagle Springs fire road, which connects East Topanga fire road with the Hub. Leaving Eagle Rock, continue down East Topanga fire road to the junction with Eagle Springs Road. Sign: *0.3 to Eagle Springs, 0.6 to Eagle Rock. Left takes you back to the Hub.*

Temescal/Trailer Canyons

Mileage: 5.4 miles one way.
Level of Difficulty: Moderate.

0.0 mile: The Hub. At mile 0.5 a sign on the left reads: *Rogers Road.* Bear right at another sign: *Conference Grounds 4.4 miles.* A firebreak trail on the left at mile 0.6 leads to one of highest points in Topanga. Leave your bike below and walk up for the view. At 3.0, go through gate to the fork at 3.1. Go right on Trailer. (Left goes to Temescal—*no bikes.*) *This is a long, steep, rutted downhill, so control your speed.*

At 4.6 miles is a closed fire gate. At 5.4 miles and another closed fire gate, you leave the dirt. This is a short driveway-type entrance at Michael Drive, where a sign reads: *Topanga*

"Walk bike" section of Rogers Road Trail at Chicken Ridge and Gobbler's Knob. Mountain Bike Unit volunteers frequently monitor this section of trail.

State Park, Trailer Canyon Entrance. Go right on Michael Drive, then left at the T intersection on Vereda de la Montura. Go a half-block and turn

right on Palisades Drive where there is a deli with restrooms and water. Descend to Sunset Boulevard. Turn right to the ocean and PCH.

Natoma Fire Road

Mileage: 0.75 mile one way.
Level of Difficulty: Moderate to steep climb.
Access: Natoma. Head south (toward the hills) on Serania (DeSoto) at Ventura Boulevard and continue through the stop sign at Dumetz where it becomes Wells Drive. Follow Wells around, passing the stop sign at Westchester County on the right. Turn right on Natoma and take it to the end where it turns to dirt. Park here.

0.0 mile: Steep climb. The road forks just past mile 0.3; go left and you come to Mulholland Drive at about mile 0.8. (Across the intersection is Santa Maria Road, which drops down to Topanga; right goes to Canoga Avenue.) Turn left on Dirt Mulholland, and look out for OHVs. Mile 1.37 marks the junction with Winnetka fire road on the left (north) which drops back down to San Fernando Valley. Go straight. Winnetka was paved at one time, so there's tons of junk, and it forks and reconnects.

There's a steep climb.

Mile 1.5 marks another junction, with the right fork signed: *Santa Monica Mountains Conservancy.* Go straight.

On the left (north) at mile 1.8 is Gleneagles fire gate, an easy beginner access to Dirt Mulholland. (To get to Gleneagles, take Van Alden Boulevard south across Ventura Boulevard. Just before the dead-end and berms, turn right on Gleneagles Street, then left on Greenbriar to a locked fire gate at the cul-de-sac.)

Giving directions, Rogers Road Trail in Topanga State Park, just north of Will Rogers State Historic Park.

Continue straight. A sign on the right (south) marks *Restricted Entry.* *Note:* The Santa Monica Mountains Conservancy is currently developing this area as park land, and future use is uncertain. At mile 2.3 you pass a water tower on the right (south). Just before mile 3, you come to fire road #30 on the right (south), the entrance to Topanga State Park.

TOPANGA STATE PARK

Best **Access**: Trippet Ranch. From San Fernando Valley go south on Topanga Canyon Boulevard. From the top of Topanga, 4.3 miles, turn left on Entrada and proceed uphill to Topanga State Park. Stay on Entrada, passing two lower lots. At the junction, bear left on Entrada, left into the parking area, and pay a $5 day-use fee. At the fire road entrance on the southeast end of the parking lot a sign reads: *2 miles to Eagle Rock, 2.2 to Waterfall Santa Inez Trail* [closed to bikes], *4.8 to Mulholland* [fire road #30], *8 miles to Temescal Conference Grounds, 8.7 miles to Will Rogers* [closed to bikes], *3 miles to Parker Mesa Overlook* [south], *4.8 Pacific Palisades* [Paseo Miramar].

Trippet Ranch/East Topanga Loop

Mileage: 18-mile loop.
Level of Difficulty: Very difficult.

This 18-mile ride with plenty of climbing for intermediate to expert cyclists includes Eagle Springs, the Hub, Trailer Canyon and Paseo Miramar.

0.0 mile: Leave parking lot. Go left (north) at a T. At 1.3 miles there is a three-way fork. *(No bikes allowed on the left fork, Musch Trail.)* Trippet Ranch Trail on the middle fork climbs to Eagle Rock (0.6 mile). The right fork descends to Eagle Springs (0.3 mile). Take this right descent down to Eagle Springs and then climb to the Hub at mile 2.0. Head right (south) on East Temescal fire road. At mile 5.0, go through the fire gate and on to the junction of Temescal and Trailer canyons (left is Temescal, and the trail is closed to bikes farther down). Turn right on Trailer Canyon, a long, steep, rutted downhill. *Control your speed.* At 6.6 miles go through a closed fire gate and continue descend-ing to mile 7.4. Go through another closed fire gate and leave the dirt. This is a short cul-de-sac at Michael Drive; the sign reads *Topanga State Park, Trailer Canyon Entrance.*

Turn right on Michael Drive and left at the T intersection at Vereda de la Montura. Go a half-block and turn right on Palisades Drive (deli with restrooms and water). Descend to mile 10.55; turn right on Sunset Boulevard. At mile 10.7, turn right on Paseo Miramar. Dig in, it's a climb! Follow the yellow lines in the road to the fire road entrance at 12.0 miles. Continue climbing. The junction with Parker Mesa Overlook fire road is at 14.2 miles. For a short out and back with nice views, turn left and go a half-mile to a dead-end overlook. At mile 15.2 return to the junction. Go straight on East Topanga fire road back to Trippet Ranch parking lot at mile 18.

CHAPTER 3

Topanga Canyon to Las Virgenes/ Malibu Canyon

Several old fire roads cut through the Topanga and Calabasas hills. Development has eliminated or cut off many of the through routes, but you may ride dirt for many miles in this east-west corridor and see some spectacular peaks and beautiful sandstone formations. Mule deer are frequently seen along the trails.

Micky McTigue

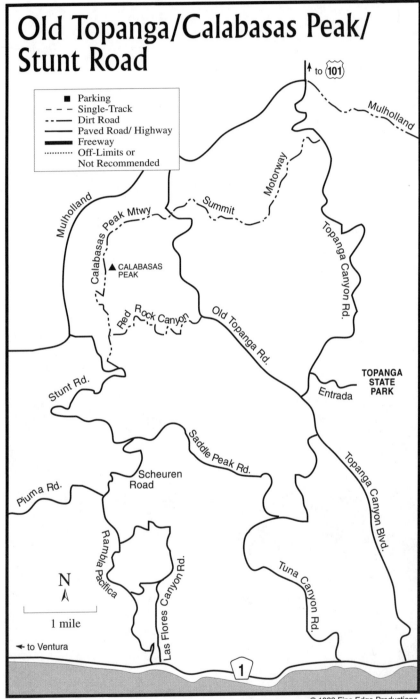

Old Topanga/Calabasas Peak/ Stunt Road

Parking
- - - Single-Track
-·-·- Dirt Road
——— Paved Road/ Highway
▬▬▬ Freeway
·········· Off-Limits or Not Recommended

to 101
Mulholland
Mulholland
Motorway
Summit
Calabasas Peak Mtwy
▲ CALABASAS PEAK
Red Rock Canyon
Old Topanga Rd.
Topanga Canyon Rd.
TOPANGA STATE PARK
Stunt Rd.
Entrada
Saddle Peak Rd.
Scheuren Road
Piuma Rd.
Rambla Pacifica
Las Flores Canyon Rd.
Tuna Canyon Rd.
Topanga Canyon Blvd.

N
1 mile
← to Ventura

1

© 1998 Fine Edge Productions

Here, too, you may notice the clash between modern development and some more traditional mountain and canyon dwellers. Neither the more affluent newcomers nor the older recluses are very fond of mountain bicyclists, so be courteous. *Caution: This area of the mountains gets a great deal of equestrian use.*

Summit Motorway

Mileage: 2.9 miles one way.
Level of Difficulty: Generally easy with a steep descent.
Access: Old Topanga Road Summit

This short east-west fire road connects Old Topanga Road with Topanga Canyon Boulevard at Entrado Road (not to be confused with Entrada to the south and east by Topanga State Park). From the summit of Old Topanga Road set your odometer to 0.0 mile and head east on the fire road from the water tower across the street from the Calabasas Peak Motorway. It is a wide, smooth dirt road. Turn left at the fork at mile 0.9.

At 1.6 miles you cross a private road (Henry Ridge), and continue straight. At 2.1 miles, begin a very steep descent to Alto Drive (blacktop). Turn left at mile 2.6 on Entrado. Topanga Canyon Boulevard is at mile 2.9. *Watch out for dogs!*

Red Rock/Calabasas Peak

Mileage: 3.9 miles one way.
Level of Difficulty: Moderate to difficult.
Access: Old Boy Scout Camp on Red Rock Road off Old Topanga Road. From the north, take Old Topanga Road 4 miles south of Mulholland Highway. Cross the bridge over a creek and turn right on Red Rock Road. Proceed 0.8 miles on a single lane, undeveloped road to a chained gate at the Santa Monica Mountains Conservancy sign and park here. From the south, take Pacific Coast Highway to Topanga Canyon Boulevard. Proceed 4.5 miles and turn left on Old Topanga Road. Go 2.0 miles and turn left on Red Rock Road.

This is one of the most beautiful and unusual sandstone canyons in the Santa Monicas. It climbs from the Boy Scout Camp to Calabasas Peak Motorway, which connects Stunt Road with Calabasas Peak and Old Topanga Road.

At 0.0 mile you pass a ranch house on the left. The climb is gradual, with some steep sections for 1.2 miles. Red Rock Road dead-ends at Calabasas Peak Motorway. To the right it's a very steep climb to Cal-

abasas Peak (mile 2.3) and then a descent to Old Topanga Road (mile 3.9) near the summit by the water tower and *Summit Motorway*. If you go left at the junction of Calabasas Peak Motorway and Red Rock, you descend steeply 0.6 mile to Stunt Road at the parking pullout for the Stunt Nature Trail, which is *closed to bicycles*. It's part of the beautiful Cold Creek Canyon preserve, and even hikers need reservations to access this area. Stash your bike and take a hike!

MBU in action, Topanga State Park at the Hub.

Mark Langton

CHAPTER 4

Las Virgenes/ Malibu Canyon to Kanan-Dume

*Malibu Creek State Park; Corral Canyon/
Mesa Peak/Puerco Canyon; Solstice Canyon/
Latigo Backbone Trail; Cheeseboro Canyon Park;
Palo Comado/China Flats/Oak Park;
Paramount Ranch*

MALIBU CREEK STATE PARK

Access: Park entrance at Mulholland and Las Virgines. Take Freeway 101 to Las Virgines-Malibu Canyon. Go south 3 miles, cross Mulholland, and continue 0.3 mile to the park entrance on the right ($5 day-use fee). There is parking outside the entrance. You can also access Malibu Creek State Park via the Liberty Canyon and Grasslands trails. To access the Liberty Canyon Trail, travel north on 101 past Las Virgenes Road/Malibu Canyon Road to Liberty Canyon Road, go south (left) approximately one mile to the intersection of Liberty Canyon and Park Vista. There is a black wrought iron fence with a walk through that passes between some houses and horse stables. The Grasslands Trail crosses Mulholland Drive about a quarter-mile north of Las Virgenes Road. You can park along Mulholland and access Malibu Creek via the Grasslands Trail. The trail starts with a horse walkover next to a private driveway. There is also access to Malibu Creek on Crags Drive: From Lake Vista Drive off Mulholland Highway, turn on Crags Drive to the Park boundary. Within

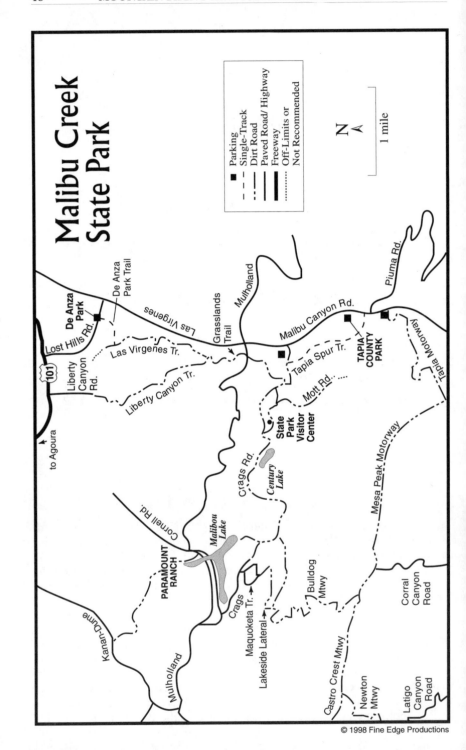

Malibu Creek State Park

Parking
Single-Track
Dirt Road
Paved Road/Highway
Freeway
Off-Limits or
Not Recommended

N

1 mile

Main entrance to Malibu Creek State Park from Las Virgenes Canyon Road.

0.8 mile you come to a parking area. A sign at the park gate reads *Bulldog Motorway*. Another alternative access point is from Juan Bautista De Anza Park in Calabasas, off Lost Hills Road. Take Malibu Canyon-Las Virgenes Road from the 101 freeway, turn right on Lost Hills Road. De Anza Park is on your left (you must go to the next stop sign and make a U-turn to access the parking lot). The De Anza Park Trail runs out the back of the park and is a fun 0.4 of a mile over to Las Virgenes Trail.

Malibu Creek State Park, one of the three large State Parks in the mountains, offers connecting trails from the coast to the south and west. The variety of terrain and natural features enables bicyclists to enjoy a diversity of riding experiences. There are suitable rides in this area for mountain bicyclists of all levels.

Traveling south on Las Virgenes Road from Freeway 101, you can imagine what were once unspoiled views of the mountains. The land adjacent to the road was slated to be acquired for park land, but when funds were not available, much of it was developed as high-density housing. This is a clear example of the "condominimization" of the mountains, a pattern that now threatens the north slopes of the Santa Monicas along the 101 corridor from Calabasas to Point Mugu.

The Visitor's Center at Malibu Creek State Park has fascinating exhibits that document past uses of the park land, an area rich in history. A year-round stream that cuts through Malibu Gorge has always supported a bountiful plant and wildlife population. Human habitation dates back at least 5,000 years. The Chumash Indians had their largest Santa Monica Mountains settlement near here.

Later, in the Mexican rancho days, the valleys and grasslands were used for cattle grazing.

The property was later developed as the Crags Country Club, a private hunting and fishing club. Century Lake was built in 1901 for the members, some of whom built small houses here as weekend retreats. The ruins of one home, the John Mott adobe, can still be seen. The area was then acquired as the 20th Century Movie Ranch. Dozens of films were made here since the variety of terrain and plant life allowed filmmakers to recreate settings from around the world. In addition to many westerns, the 20th Century Ranch simulated Africa in several Tarzan movies. Perhaps its most famous set was for the television series "M*A*S*H." Some of you may remember an episode in which the 4077th returned to the smoldering remains of their camp. The episode was filmed after a terrible brush fire swept the park in 1982. Now all that remains of the "M*A*S*H" site are a couple of rusty jeeps.

Today, Malibu Creek State Park is used by bicyclists, hikers, equestrians, fishermen, picnickers and, most recently, campers who come to enjoy its rugged character. The Grotto and Century Lake are rich with bass. This much water is rare in the Santa Monicas, so unusual plant and animal life abound. The trails on the floor of the park are generally flat, inviting users of all levels, but the trails that climb to Castro Crest are steep and demanding. Because the park is so heavily used, bicyclists should always *use extra caution.*

Liberty Canyon Trail

Mileage: 1.46 miles.
Level of Difficulty: Easy with one short, steep singletrack.

At the wrought iron fence at Liberty Canyon and Park Vista, set your odometer at mile 0.0. Go through the walk-through and continue down the paved road 0.3 mile to the end. The trail is on the left. This trail takes you over to the park entrance. Go right onto Liberty Canyon Trail (fire road). Liberty Canyon Trail rolls gently alongside Medea Creek. At mile 0.7 you see a fence and ranch ahead of you, and a singletrack trail snaking up to your left. This is the only way around the privately inheld ranch property and is okay to use.

When you get to the top of the short hill you can turn right down along the fence, or go left and continue on the short singletrack around the big oak tree to the main fire road. Continue left to the intersection of Liberty Canyon Trail and Grasslands Trail (1.46 miles). (About 0.3 mile before you get to the Grasslands Trail intersection, the Talopop Trail joins the Liberty Canyon Trail on the left. This climbs steeply for about 0.5 mile until it reaches the ridge that looks down onto Las Virgenes Road. The singletrack trail is off limits to bikes, yet is very seldom used. It connects with the Las Virgenes Trail).

Grasslands Trail

Mileage: 1.47 miles from Liberty Canyon Trail to Crags Drive in Malibu Creek, 2.8 miles when used in conjunction with Liberty Canyon Trail as access from Liberty Canyon to Malibu Creek State Park; 0.73 mile from Mulholland to Liberty Canyon Trail; 0.74 mile from Mulholland to Crags in Malibu Creek State Park.
Level of Difficulty: Easy to moderate.

The Grassland Trail merges with the Liberty Canyon Trail 1.46 miles from Liberty Canyon. To continue on to Malibu Creek State Park, turn right. You go over a creek and then up a short hill to a sharp left hairpin turn. Continue on the fire road until you come to the Crater Substation paved drive; turn right. Just a few yards up the drive, turn left onto the trail and continue on the Grasslands Trail around the substation and along a barbed wire fence. Soon you come to Mulholland Drive. Crossing Mulholland and just to the right is the Grasslands Trail connector into Malibu Creek State Park. Continuing on the Grasslands Trail you head up a short steep hill and onto a ridge where you can see the parking lots, Hunter House, and ranger kiosk on the left (south), and Malibu Creek State Park on the right (north). Stay on the Grasslands Trail; do not take any spur trails. *Please use caution since this trail gets a lot of equestrian use.* The Grasslands Trail quickly takes you down to the main Malibu Creek access road (Crags Road) just before the concrete bridge over Malibu Creek. Turn right here to go toward Bulldog Motorway.

To access the Grasslands Trail from Malibu Creek State Park main parking lot, travel 0.2 mile from parking lot on Crags Road; the Grasslands Trail trailhead will be on your right.

Las Virgenes Trail

Mileage: 1.28 miles.
Level of Difficulty: Moderate.

The Las Virgenes Trail continues from the Liberty Canyon Trail and Grasslands Trail intersection. If you are coming from Liberty Canyon, continue straight; from Grasslands (Mulholland) merge right. Continue 0.2 mile to a left-hand turn (to the right is White Oak Farm, a private residence). You are now on a rolling doubletrack with Las Virgenes Road to your right. At 1.28 miles you come to a T. To the left is the Talopop Trail, which is technically off limits to bikes as it is in a grasslands preserve. Straight ahead is the park boundary and a system of fire roads that will take you over to a housing tract development. To the right is the De Anza Park Trail, a short (0.33 mile) but fun trail that ends in the back of City of Calabasas' Juan Bautista De Anza Park at Lost Hills Road. This is a good alternative if you choose not to ride back on the Las Virgenes Trail. Ride over to De Anza Park and out to Lost Hills Road, turn right to Las Virgenes Road, then right to the entrance to Malibu Creek State Park. Please note that traffic can be heavy on this section of Las Virgenes Road.

Crags Road

Mileage: 3.4 miles one way.
Level of Difficulty: Easy to moderate, depending on condition of creek bed.

At the lower parking lot by the restrooms, set your odometer to 0.0. Take the road signed *Authorized Vehicles Only,* cross a concrete bridge, and begin Crags Road, which here in the park is dirt. At mile 1.7 cross another bridge and continue on the main trail. At mile 2.4, Lost Cabin Trail on the left is marked by an Indian mortar rock. (Lost Cabin goes 0.7 mile to a dead end). Next you ride through a burned-out set of the television series "M*A*S*H." You'll recognize the mountains as those in

helicopter scenes in the opening credits of the series. At mile 2.7 go right at the fork (left is Bulldog Motorway, marked by a sign that reads *Park Boundary 4.3 Miles, Castro Peak Motorway 3.4 miles*). Within 0.4 mile you come to another fork. Go left here, and continue about 0.3 mile to Crags Drive at the park boundary. (A right takes you 0.3 mile to a dead end at another park boundary and the waterfall end of Malibu Lake. The lake is private and not accessible.)

Bulldog Loop/Lakeside Lateral Loop/ Lookout Loop

Mileage: 12-mile or 14.7-mile loop.
Level of Difficulty: Difficult.

Bulldog is a tough climb to the ridge of Castro Crest and Mesa Peak. Once there, fire roads go west toward Latigo Canyon, east to Mesa Peak and Tapia Natural Area County Park, and south toward Puerco Canyon. There is a parking lot near the top of Bulldog that can be reached by Corral Canyon off Pacific Coast Highway (see below).

Bulldog Motorway intersects Crags Road 0.3 mile past the M*A*S*H site at about 2.7 miles (starting mileage at Malibu Creek State Park main parking lot). Turn left (south) uphill. At mile 4.0 bear left. (To the right begins the Lakeside Lateral fire road/Lookout Loop described at the end of this ride.)

Mile 6.4 marks the top of Bulldog and the junction with Castro Crest

Motorway. Right goes to antenna towers on Castro Peak and descends via Newton or Brewster motorways to Latigo Canyon (see description below).This is also the way you would reach the Solstice Canyon/ Latigo section of the Backbone singletrack. (See accompanying description below for the Solstice Canyon/Latigo Backbone Trail.)

Turn left and descend to 7.2 miles to the Corral Canyon parking lot, continuing through the parking lot and out onto the pavement. Watch for a fire road on the left just past mile 7.5. There is a wooden fence where telephone wires cross the road. Turn left on the fire road (Mesa Peak Motorway), which has several good climbs, and descends to a fork at 10.2

miles with Puerco Canyon on the right. Go left at the fork.

In a short distance, Mesa Peak fire road begins its descent to Malibu Canyon, away from the ocean. At mile 12.0 there is a hairpin right turn at a chain link fence and the trail forks. Bear right up a little hill. The next half-mile is steep and rocky in places, so use extra caution. At mile 12.7, just before the trail intersects Malibu Canyon Road (you'll be able to see the road below you), a single-track trail comes in from the left. You can either take the singletrack down into the parking lot or Malibu Canyon Road. It is safer to stay on dirt as much as possible. In either case, you will be heading north (away from the ocean) on Malibu Canyon Road for a short distance over to Tapia Park to access the Tapia Spur Trail back into Malibu Creek State Park.

Turning left onto the singletrack, descend 100 yards to a T, then turn right to Malibu Canyon Road and the parking lot. Turn left (north) and go across the bridge. Just on the other side of the bridge is the entrance to Tapia Park (a sub-unit of Malibu Creek State Park), at mile 13.0. (Tapia Park itself has only paved roads and picnic areas, no trail system except Tapia Spur Trail into Malibu Creek State Park.)

As you enter Tapia Park, turn right and

go past the ranger kiosk to the next left, toward the Salvation Army Camp, about a half-mile. Go all the way to just before the entrance to the camp; the Tapia Spur Trail entrance will be on your right, mile 13.9. At mile 14.3 you come to a saddle overlooking Malibu Creek State Park. Continue on until the trail drops you into the park, merging with with Group Camp access road just past mile 14.7. The main paved road is just ahead and will take you back to the main lower parking lot.

For the Lakeside Lateral/Lookout Loop, turn right at the Lakeside Lateral fire road at the junction 1.3 miles from the beginning of Bulldog Loop. Climb the short hill and turn right at the top. This takes you over

Upper Plateau, Los Robles Trail.

Mark Langton

to Lookout Road which descends back to paved Crags Road and the park entrance. It is a good alternate route if you want to add a little distance to the Crags Road-Malibu Creek route or don't want to do the entire Bulldog Loop. Be careful as you descend after rolling for about three-quarters of a mile. The fire road gets very steep and, depending on the time of year, can either be extremely rutted, loose, rocky, or all of the above.

At mile 2.1 you come to the park boundary and pavement. Continue downhill on Lookout and follow it all the way down to Crags Road, or go down the Maquoketah Trail (paved) which winds over to Lookout where you turn left to Crags. Turn right on Crags to the park entrance. Total distance of Lakeside Lateral/Lookout Loop from Bulldog is 3.2 miles.

CORRAL CANYON/MESA PEAK/ PUERCO CANYON

Access: Corral Canyon parking lot. On Pacific Coast Highway 2.4 miles west of Malibu Canyon Road, turn right on Corral Canyon Road and climb 5.3 miles to a gravel parking lot. Look left (west) to Bulldog and Latigo Canyon; north to Malibu Creek State Park. If you're riding Puerco, it's a good idea to drop a car at the bottom of Puerco Canyon, half-way between Malibu Canyon Road and Corral Canyon. Park where Puerco turns to dirt.

Castro Crest, Newton and Brewster Motorways

Mileage: 3.5 miles one way.
Level of Difficulty: Difficult.

0.0 mile: Head west from Corral Canyon parking lot and climb through the fire gate to mile 1.0 and the junction of Bulldog and Castro Crest. Bear left. (Right is Bulldog which drops down to Malibu Creek State Park.) Climb to Castro Peak at mile 1.6. Just before the peak is the junction with Newton Motorway on the left. It climbs briefly, then descends to Latigo Canyon Road, total mileage 1.75 miles. The Latigo Canyon Road-Newton Motorway trailhead (at a wrought iron sign for a private home that reads "Hellacious Acres") is approximately seven miles from Pacific Coast Highway.

If you want to access the Solstice Canyon/Latigo Backbone Trail, turn left at the intersection of Castro Crest and Newton motorways. After a short climb, you descend to a saddle at approximately mile 1.0. There are trail markers and singletrack trail entrances on both the right and left. This is the Solstice Canyon/Latigo Backbone Trail as it crosses over Newton Motorway. A right turn (west) takes you to

Latigo Canyon Road; a left turn takes you to Corral Canyon parking lot at Mesa Peak Motorway (see Solstice Canyon/Latigo Backbone Trail for mileages).

If you stay on Castro Crest Motorway rather than taking Newton Motorway to the Backbone Trail, the route descends past Castro Peak about 1.75 miles to a junction with Upper Brewster Motorway. Left drops down to Latigo Canyon. Right continues to Mulholland Highway just east of Kanan-Dume Road.

Puerco Canyon and Mesa Peak Motorway

Mileage: 6.9 miles one way.
Level of Difficulty: Difficult.

0.0 mile: Corral Canyon parking lot. Head east back out the road for about 0.3 mile until a telephone line crosses the road. Turn left at the wooden gate onto a fire road. Proceed 3 miles to the junction of Puerco (on right) and Mesa Peak Motorway (detailed above in the Bulldog Loop ride). From here, Puerco is a long, beautiful descent. Turn right on Puerco and go through a second gate at mile 3.6. Puerco descends steeply another 3.3 miles.

Solstice Canyon/Latigo/ Zuma Canyon Backbone Trail

Mileage: 6.5 miles one way.
Difficulty: Very difficult.
Access: From the Ventura Freeway 101, go south 7.8 miles on Kanan-Dume to the third tunnel. The parking lot is on the right just before tunnel. From Pacific Coast Highway, go north on Kanan-Dume 4.3 miles to the first tunnel ("Tunnel One"); the parking lot is just on the other side of tunnel on the left. To access the ride from Corral Canyon at Mesa Peak Motorway, see Corral Canyon/Mesa Peak/Puerco Canyon in this chapter. (Note: Do not leave valuables in car in the Corral Canyon parking lot; it has been the site of several thefts.) To get to the Zuma Ridge Motorway entrance to the Zuma Canyon section of the Backbone Trail, take Kanan-Dume (from either the 101 freeway or PCH) to Mulholland Highway, go west to the split, left on Encinal Canyon about a mile. Zuma Ridge Motorway comes in from the left just after Camp Kilpatrick. There is a sign that says "Buzzard's Roost." There is turnout parking just past the entrance to the motorway.

The Solstice Canyon/Latigo Backbone Trail, in NPS property, was opened up largely by the efforts of CORBA. It is virtually all single-track—very technical, with steep pitches, rocky outcroppings, deeply rutted sections, and several steam crossings. For the beginning rider it is not recommended; for the intermediate rider, it is a challenge; for the advanced rider, it is pure fun.

There are two ways to ride the Solstice Canyon/Latigo Backbone Trail, out and back from either the Kanan-Dume trailhead at Tunnel One or from Corral Canyon parking

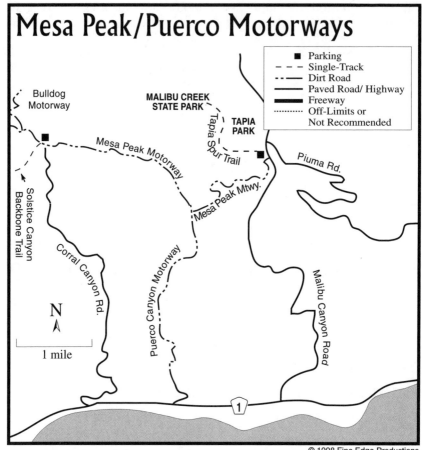

Mesa Peak/Puerco Motorways

■ Parking
– – – Single-Track
·–·–· Dirt Road
——— Paved Road/ Highway
——— Freeway
··········· Off-Limits or Not Recommended

Bulldog Motorway

MALIBU CREEK STATE PARK

Tapia Spur Trail

TAPIA PARK

Mesa Peak Motorway

Mesa Peak Mtwy.

Piuma Rd.

Solstice Canyon Backbone Trail

Corral Canyon Rd.

Puerco Canyon Motorway

Malibu Canyon Road

N

1 mile

1

© 1998 Fine Edge Productions

lot at Mesa Peak Motorway. Both are equally challenging and offer excellent examples of the area's riparian oak habitat. Access is quite a bit easier from Kanan-Dume Road since there is less mountain road driving.

Even though it is only six miles one way, this route is an all-encompassing ride that will challenge even the best riders. For additional mileage you can ride over to Puerco Canyon via Mesa Peak Motorway.

In mid-1998, an extension of the Backbone Trail was completed between Tunnel One and Zuma Ridge Motorway, with still more of the Backbone being built to the north. While parking is limited at Zuma Ridge Motorway where it meets Encinal Canyon Road, this is an excellent stretch of singletrack that adds 2.6 miles (one-way) to this section of Backbone Trail. You can either park at Encinal Canyon Road and Zuma Ridge Motorway and do the entire route section to Corral Canyon parking lot out and back, or start at Tunnel One and do the Zuma Canyon section out and back, then the Latigo/Solstice Canyon section to Corral Canyon parking lot out and back. Ride up Zuma Ridge

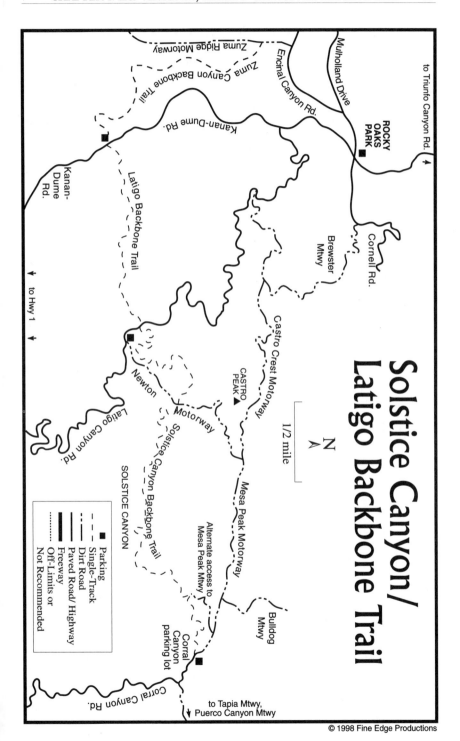

Solstice Canyon/
Latigo Backbone Trail

© 1998 Fine Edge Productions

Motorway 0.7 mile and look for trail entrance to the left.

Mileage from Kanan-Dume Road: 0.0 mile: From the parking lot at Tunnel One, the trail climbs steeply toward the coast, up to the top of the tunnel.

After climbing the steep hill, turn left and cross over the tunnel. Continue a short way to a paved drive, cross straight over, and continue to Latigo Canyon Road at 2.3 miles. (You can either go straight across to the other side of Latigo Canyon Road and through the parking lot to the continuation of the Solstice Canyon/Latigo Backbone Trail, or turn right and continue to the Hellacious Acres trailhead where Newton Motorway meets Latigo Canyon Road.) Continuing across Latigo Canyon Road, you descend into a beautiful canyon full of ferns and oak trees. As you climb out of the canyon, the trail becomes very steep and rutted, most likely requiring dismounting. After the steep section, the trail becomes more rolling and then intersects Newton Motorway at about 3.8 miles. Above you to the left is Castro Peak with its radio communication towers. Across Newton Motorway and slightly to the right is the continuation of the Backbone Trail into Solstice Canyon.

If you choose to turn right on Latigo Canyon Road instead of going across Latigo Canyon Road onto the Latigo section of the Backbone Trail, go to 2.6 miles (a wrought iron sign reads "Hellacious Acres") and turn left; continue past a fire gate marked private and begin climbing. This climb tops out and then descends quickly to a Y at mile 3.2. Take the left branch (right goes to private property; please do not trespass). At mile 3.3 you come to the intersection of the Latigo portion of the Solstice Canyon/Latigo Backbone Trail from Latigo Canyon on the left, and the Solstice Canyon portion as it comes from Corral Canyon at Mesa Peak Motorway on the right.

After crossing Newton Motorway, continue back on the singletrack (turn right if you came from Hellacious Acres). *Be careful!* This trail is very narrow in some places and can be very rutted as well. There are also four tight switchbacks as you descend into the canyon, one of which is very eroded. Once you drop into the canyon bottom, the terrain becomes rocky with several stream crossings, depending on the time of year. At about 4.8 miles you begin climbing out of the canyon and up toward Mesa Peak Motorway. Here the trail becomes more rolling, with several little steep climbs and descents. At 5.5 miles you come to a wire break dirt road. (You can go left for another short, steep climb that ascends to Mesa Peak Motorway approximately a quarter of the way to its intersection with Bulldog Motorway. Right leads to a wire tower.) Continue straight on the wide dirt road to go to the Corral Canyon parking lot. In just 0.1 mile (at about 5.6 miles) the singletrack comes back in on the left and continues to Corral Canyon parking lot, 6.5 miles. (Mileage without the middle Latigo section of the Backbone singletrack is just over 6.0 miles.)

Mileage From Corral Canyon parking lot: Mile 0.0: Descend the switchbacks and turn right onto a wide dirt road that comes in at about mile 0.5. When you come to another wide dirt road, continue straight onto a singletrack. This trail is rolling, with several short climbs and descents. At 1.3 miles you reach the canyon bottom. After several stream crossings you climb four sharp switchbacks and then reach Newton Motorway at 2.7 miles. From here you can continue straight across to the middle Latigo singletrack section of the Backbone Trail or you can turn left and take Newton Motorway toward the coast to Latigo Canyon Road 0.7 miles farther.

For the Newton Motorway option, you climb a bit before turning right just past the gate at a Y, away from private property. At 3.4 miles you come to Latigo Canyon Road. To get onto the remaining section of the Backbone Trail, turn right and go downhill to just past mile 3.7, where the trail comes in on the left. Take this trail back to the Kanan-Dume Tunnel One parking lot.

If you chose to stay on the Latigo section of the Backbone Trail rather than taking Newton Motorway, the trail rolls along for a mile or so before you reach a very steep, rutted descent that is quite dangerous. After the rutted section the trail drops into a lush, fern-infested canyon, then climbs back up to Latigo Canyon Road and a parking lot at mile 4.2. Go across Latigo Canyon Road to hook up with the last section of the Backbone Trail (Newton Backbone) as it descends to Kanan-Dume Road. At mile 6.0 you come to a paved drive; go straight across to the trail with the railroad ties. You will probably be able to hear traffic on Kanan-Dume at this point. At about 6.3 miles you are on top of the Tunnel One; unless you arranged a shuttle, you may want to turn around here rather than dropping down the quarter-mile into the Tunnel One parking lot. To continue on the extension of Backbone to Zuma Ridge Motorway, descend into the parking lot and turn left onto the singletrack.

Newton Motorway at the saddle between Latigo and Solstice Canyon sections of the Backbone Trail, Santa Monica Mountains National Recreation Area.

John Fisher

CHEESEBORO CANYON PARK

Access: Take Freeway 101 to the Chesebro exit (2.7 miles west of Las Virgenes Road or 2.4 miles east of Kanan-Dume Road). Head north and make a quick right on Chesebro Road. Follow the narrow street 1 mile to a right turn just before the sign: Cheeseboro Canyon. You can park here or continue up the road a quarter-mile to another larger parking lot.

Technically, Cheeseboro Canyon is not part of the Santa Monica Mountains. Since the acquisition of Palo Comado Canyon and China Flats to the west, the combined acreage makes it the largest National Park Service (NPS) holding in the Santa Monica Mountains National Recreation Area, and it is the major wildlife corridor for animals traveling from the Angeles National Forest and Santa Susanna Mountains to the Santa Monicas. NPS is very good about signing trails for approved travel. Please obey signs that indicate approved use. Part of an old cattle ranch, the area resembles Marin County—rolling hills, coastal oaks, sea breezes on the ridges and enough horse and cow plop to remind you that this is the West. Wildlife includes golden eagles, deer, bobcat, hawks, coyotes and the usual assortment of reptiles. *Caution: There are many rattlesnakes here.*

Cheeseboro Canyon has been a hotbed of political activity since it borders China Flats and Palo Camado Canyon, areas that have been sought for development for years. China Flats and

Palo Camado Canyon were owned by actor/comedian Bob Hope, and it was his dream to build a championship golf course in Palo Camado Canyon. Because this area is a major wildlife corridor, environmentalists felt that no development should take place on surrounding undeveloped

Cheeseboro Canyon, Santa Monica Mountains National Recreation Area.

Mark Langton

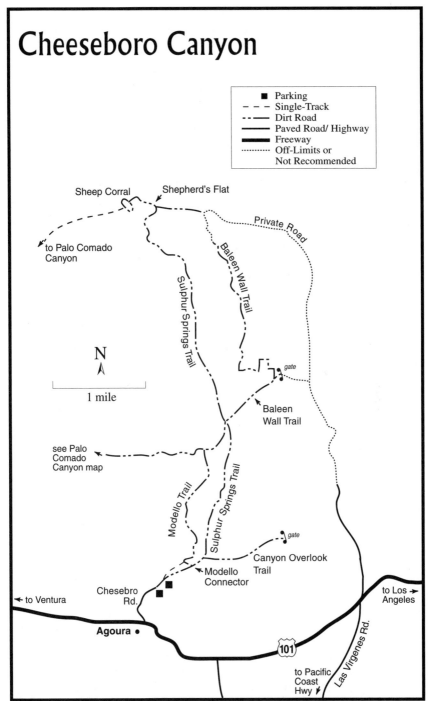

Cheeseboro Canyon

Parking
Single-Track
Dirt Road
Paved Road/ Highway
Freeway
Off-Limits or
Not Recommended

Sheep Corral   Shepherd's Flat

Private Road

to Palo Comado
Canyon

Baleen Wall Trail

Sulphur Springs Trail

N

1 mile

gate

Baleen
Wall Trail

see Palo
Comado
Canyon map

Modello Trail

Sulphur Springs Trail

gate

Canyon Overlook
Trail

Modello
Connector

Chesebro
Rd.

to Ventura

to Los
Angeles

Agoura •

101

to Pacific
Coast
Hwy

Las Virgenes Rd.

© 1998 Fine Edge Productions

acreage. These environmentalists effectively blocked the development in Palo Camado, enabling the Santa Monica Mountains Conservancy and National Park Service to purchase the area for public recreation. A new deal was structured to combine that development with another proposed residential community development east of the Cheeseboro Canyon Park boundary.

At the time of this guide's printing, the viability of that community was still being studied. Such a development would include dedicating approximately 3,000 acres of open space that would be annexed onto Cheeseboro Canyon directly to the east (Malibu Canyon) and north, much of it open and usable for mountain biking. Currently the property to the east and north of Cheeseboro Canyon remains accessible via park roads, yet it is technically private and you are subject to any enforcement deemed appropriate by law.

The main Sulphur Springs trail is a 6.25-mile out-and-back route with three offshoots. Riders on the main trail can explore the canyon bottomland which rolls through grasslands and coastal oak groves into dense chaparral. The side trails that climb to the ridges above the park afford bird's-eye views of the canyon below. You can also access Palo Comado Canyon from Cheeseboro Canyon, creating options of either a short loop using lower Palo Comado and Cheeseboro canyons, or adding a significant amount of mileage if you choose to do the entire Palo Comado/China Flats/Oak Park loop (see separate trail description).

Sulphur Springs Trail/Sheep Corral

Mileage: 12.5 miles out and back.
Level of Difficulty: Moderate.

0.0 mile: Begin at the outer gate off Chesebro Road, and proceed 0.25 mile to the other parking lot and the Sulphur Springs trail entrance. There is a bulletin board information center where you can study maps and read about the Cheeseboro Canyon's natural history. There are portapotties here, but no water is available. At mile 0.8 go straight past the first junction with Modello Trail on the left. Just before mile 1.0, you pass the junction with Canyon Overlook Trail on the right.

At 1.5 miles bear left past the Y with Baleen Wall Trail on the right. At 1.6 miles go straight at the junction with Modello Trail (on the left), and at mile 4.1 you pass the bottom of a singletrack climb to the Baleen Wall posted *No bikes*. (It is illegal to take your bike on this trail.) At mile

4.4 the road turns to singletrack and crosses a stream. On the left, just after you cross the stream you can see a rock with some interesting fossils. The singletrack follows the sometimes sandy stream bed up the canyon. There are short, steep dips and climbs and plenty of rocks on the trail. At mile 5.75 the trail comes to a T-junction and Shepherd's Flat with the right fork going approximately a quarter-mile to a dead-end turnaround. The left fork, Upper Connector, leads over to Palo Comado Canyon. In spring the area around these forks has plenty of wildflowers. Return to the Chesebro trailhead from the T, watching for Modello Trail on the right. Take it (see Modello Trail below), or continue straight to the main parking lot at mile 12.5.

Canyon Overlook Trail

Mileage: 1.4 miles out and back.
Level of Difficulty: Moderate with a steep climb near the turnaround.

At 0.96 mile from the park entrance turn right off the Sulphur Springs Trail onto Canyon Overlook Trail, which climbs steeply 0.7 mile east and then south to a hill overlooking several of the canyons and ridges of Cheeseboro Park.

When the mustard is blooming in the spring this area is carpeted in yellow. The road is quite rutted so *watch your steep downhill return* to the main Sulphur Springs Trail.

Baleen Wall Trail

Mileage: 5.4 miles out and back (7.4 miles with the service road).
Level of Difficulty: Moderate with some steep climbs.

At 1.5 miles on the Sulphur Springs Trail turn right onto the Baleen Wall Trail. Reset your odometer to 0.0 mile. Bear left past the service road at mile 0.7 on the right. (It climbs for a mile up to electric towers and great views of the canyon.)

The trail climbs steeply. At about 1.3 miles you pass a water tank on the left and head back to the north.

At 2.5 miles the road forks again; follow the main road. The hiking trail to the left is just that: *Illegal for bikes.* The road dead-ends at the last electric tower at mile 2.7 in high grass. From here, you can see the top of Baleen Wall rock formations. Return down the long descent to Sulphur Springs Trail.

Modello Trail

Mileage: 1.3 miles one way.
Level of Difficulty: Easy to moderate.

At 0.8 mile along the Sulphur Springs Trail you pass the south entrance to the Modello Trail on the left. Farther up Sulphur Springs at 1.6 miles you pass the north entrance of Modello on the left.

From the north entrance reset your odometer to 0.0 and climb 0.3 mile to a left turn on a doubletrack. The right turn takes you over to Palo Comado Canyon. Climb to the junction at mile 1.0 and turn right to descend 0.3 mile to the parking lots. (The left descends to the south junction with Sulphur Springs Trail.)

Palo Comado Access/ Lower Palo Comado Canyon Loop

Mileage: 7.6 miles.
Level of Difficulty: Moderate (some steep climbing).

Using the Modello Trail description above, take Sulphur Springs Trail to the North Modello Trail connector at 1.6 miles on your left, but do not zero out your odometer. Climb the doubletrack to the intersection of Modello Trail at 1.9 miles. Across the small valley is a fence and open gate entrance along the ridge. Bearing right, ride down the short descent and then up to the ridge, through the gate, then descend again into another deeper valley and climb on the opposite side. Stay on the main trail, a wide dirt road, as it crests yet another ridge and crosses over a saddle. Descend once more into Palo Comado Canyon. At 2.9 miles you come to the intersection of the lower Palo Comado Canyon main trail. To your left is the boundary and private property. Please do not enter or exit here. Go right up-canyon along the rolling fire road.

At 3.6 miles a fire road comes in from the left. This is an old ranch road that takes you over to

Oak Park, but it is not a main access. It does, however, lead to a ridge road that takes you back down toward where you came into Palo Camodo Canyon from Cheeseboro Canyon. Continue up Palo Comado Canyon to about 4.0 miles and a dirt road on your right. This is the middle connector between Palo Comado Canyon

Modello Trail, Cheeseboro Canyon, Santa Monica Mountains National Recreation Area.

Mark Langton

and Cheeseboro Canyon. (Ahead and to the left approximately one-tenth of a mile is the Oak Park connector dirt road that is the main access to Palo Comado from Oak Park. See Palo Comado Canyon/China Flats/Oak Park Loop description below.) To continue back to Cheeseboro Canyon, turn right and head uphill. The climb gets very steep here for approximately a half-mile. At 4.6 miles you cross over a ridge and begin descending steeply into Cheeseboro Canyon. At about 5.2 miles you intersect with Cheeseboro Canyon at Sulphur Springs Trail. Turn right and begin a gentle descent back toward the parking lot.

At 5.3 miles you come to a Y, with the right branch taking you onto a short singletrack that connects with Sulphur Springs Trail. If you go left there is a wider connector on the right in just a few yards. If you go straight at this connector, the dirt road connects with Sulphur Springs Trail approximately a half-mile down canyon. Using the singletrack connector (it's the most fun), continue down-canyon to about 6.2 miles and the north entrance to the Modello Trail. You can either climb up the 0.3 mile to the intersection and take the Modello Trail ridge route and singletrack back to the parking lot, or stay low and take the main canyon trail. Total mileage is 7.6 using the lower main canyon route.

PALO COMADO CANYON, CHINA FLAT, AND OAK CANYON REGIONAL PARK

Access: There are several points to Palo Comado Canyon and China Flat, as well as Oak Canyon Regional Park, which is part of the Rancho Simi Park and Recreation District. For purposes of simplicity, the Palo Comado Canyon/China Flat area will be described as a loop beginning in Oak Park, using Palo Comado Canyon from Oak Park as the main entrance.

You can access China Flat without climbing up Palo Comado Canyon by using the following directions: From the Ventura Freeway 101, exit Lindero Canyon Road and go east to the intersection of Lindero Canyon Road and Kanan Road. Continue on Lindero Canyon Road almost one mile to King James Circle, turn left, and go to the cul-de-sac. The trail for China Flat, referred to by the locals as "Dead Cow," originates here. It is a very technical, strenuous 1.7-mile climb, but the reward is the beautiful oak-studded meadows of China Flat. Parking is limited on King James, so

there are signs directing you to alternate parking on Lindero Canyon Road. There you find another trailhead between King James and Wembley. This trail is not recommended, since it is very steep and technical with much portaging. If you park on Lindero Canyon Road, ride back up King James and use the trailhead that originates at the cul-de-sac.

To access the trails in the Oak Park area, take Lindero Canyon Road off the Ventura Freeway 101 east to Kanan Road, turn right onto Holly Tree Drive, and turn left into Oak Canyon Regional Park. Take the

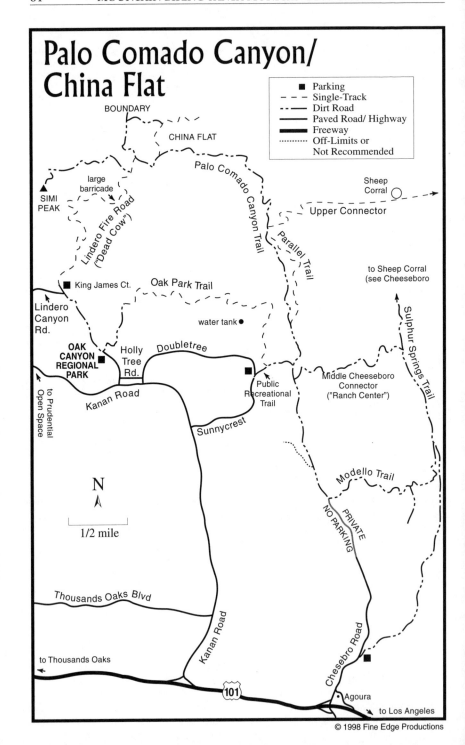

Palo Comado Canyon/ China Flat

Legend:
- ■ Parking
- – – – Single-Track
- – · – · Dirt Road
- —— Paved Road/ Highway
- ▬▬ Freeway
- ·········· Off-Limits or Not Recommended

BOUNDARY

CHINA FLAT

Palo Comado Canyon Trail

large barricade

SIMI PEAK

Lindero Fire Road ("Dead Cow")

Sheep Corral

Upper Connector

to Sheep Corral (see Cheeseboro

Parallel Trail

King James Ct.

Oak Park Trail

Lindero Canyon Rd.

water tank ●

Sulphur Springs Trail

OAK CANYON REGIONAL PARK

Holly Tree Rd.

Doubletree

to Prudential Open Space

Kanan Road

Public Recreational Trail

Middle Cheeseboro Connector ("Ranch Center")

Sunnycrest

Modello Trail

N

1/2 mile

NO PARKING   PRIVATE

Thousands Oaks Blvd

Kanan Road

Chesebro Road

to Thousands Oaks

101

Agoura

to Los Angeles

© 1998 Fine Edge Productions

driveway up to the first parking lot on the left. On your right is a driveway that leads to a house, and at the back of the driveway is the trailhead. You can see the main trail leading up into the hills along a small ridge to your left as you face the driveway.

To access Palo Comado Canyon/China Flat/Oak Park loop from Oak Park: From Ventura Freeway 101, take Kanan Road north two miles past several traffic signals to a stop sign. The next street is Sunnycrest Drive, where you turn right and follow up and around until you get to the second lefthand curve, 2.9 miles from the freeway. On your right is the Public Recreational Trail entrance with a cable barricade (marked with an *Off-road Vehicles Prohibited* sign). This curve is where Sunnycrest turns into Doubletree Drive. Parking is available

all along the street. (For a longer ride incorporating the Palo Comado Canyon/China Flat/Oak Park loop, see Palo Comado Access/Lower Palo Comado Canyon Loop in the Cheeseboro Canyon description.)

Palo Comado Canyon and China Flat are wonderful examples of community activism and political vision. At one point, it looked as though this beautiful oak-lined canyon and rugged mountain meadow would be lost to developers. But tenacious environmentalists and creative politicians, along with the Santa Monica Mountains Conservancy and National Park Service, enabled the area to be saved in 1993, effectively doubling the area of Cheeseboro Canyon and making it the largest NPS-held parcel in the Santa Monica Mountains National Recreation Area.

Palo Comado Canyon/China Flat/Oak Park Loop

Mileage: 9.6 miles.
Difficulty: Moderate to very difficult with some very technical singletrack.

Mile 0.0: From Doubletree/Sunnycrest, take Public Recreational Trail down into Palo Comado Canyon. You come to a T just short of 0.5 mile. Turn left up canyon.

(If you want to access Cheeseboro Canyon, turn right and go 0.1 mile to a dirt road on your left, which takes you over to the Sulphur Springs Trail. See Cheeseboro Canyon area description for details.) The Palo Comado Canyon Trail begins climbing more steeply at 1.3 miles. At mile 1.4 a trail comes in on the right—a moderately technical singletrack that climbs and parallels the Palo Comado Canyon

Trail. It is locally known as the Parallel Trail.

Mileage and directions are as follows for the Parallel Trail spur: Begin climbing; then at about 0.6 mile from the beginning of the spur (nearly 2.0 miles from your car) you can see the Baleen Wall to the right in Cheeseboro Canyon. At 0.7 mile (2.1 miles from your car) you come to a reverse Y where you bear left. About 50 yards farther is another Y and the Upper Connector Trail over to Cheeseboro Canyon. (See next paragraph for Connector mileage.) Almost immediately you come to a T. To the right is the preferred route which takes you to the main trail and is much more rideable. Just before mile 0.9, mile you pop out onto the Palo Comado Canyon Trail. Total mileage from the car at this point is 2.28 miles.

If you continue on the main Palo Comado Canyon Trail instead of riding the Parallel Trail from the bottom, at mile 2.16 you come to where the Parallel Trail reenters the main trail. This is also the entrance to the Upper Connector Trail into Cheeseboro Canyon. Mileage is as follows for this fun and moderately technical singletrack. At 2.3 miles you come to a Y. Take the left trail uphill for a short distance (right takes you to the Parallel Trail descent). You then round an uphill corner and promptly begin descending into a narrow canyon. The trail dips and rolls, and finally comes to an old sheep corral at mile 3.0 (0.8 mile from the Palo Comado fire road). Continue on this singletrack for about 0.1 mile to a singletrack that enters from the right. Going straight takes you, with very little technical riding, to Shepherd's Flat, while the right trail is more technical and more fun. Mileage to Shepherd's Flat taking the right trail is almost 1.2 miles from Palo Comado fire road, or a total of 3.3 miles from Oak Park.

Continuing up Palo Comado Canyon Trail, you pass active springs; even in summer the ground may be wet. Climb steeply to almost 3.1 miles, then descend a short hill to an old horse corral. From here there are two ways to access China Flat. The best way is to turn right at the old corral. If you continue on the main dirt road, it will loop around and come up to China Flat from the opposite direction. This is also the more direct route for reaching the

old Lindero Fire Road that leads down to north Oak Park and King James Court.

Turning right at the old corral, climb a short hill and then cruise over to a scenic oak-filled meadow at 3.3 miles. Bear right at the Y to continue around the perimeter of this meadow and the scrub-covered mound hill directly in front of you. At 3.5 miles, a narrow trail comes in from the right. This is a fun little singletrack that takes you 0.5 mile out and back for an additional mile of riding.

Continuing on the oak meadow perimeter trail, you come to an intersection at 3.7 miles. This is the termination of the main Palo Comado Canyon Trail (had you gone straight instead of right at the old corral). The trail directly ahead of you makes a short loop to a scenic overlook. To the right is the park boundary and private property. Turn left (downhill) at the intersection and ride to the 3.8-mile point, where the previously mentioned scenic loop trail comes back down, as does an alternate connector to the Simi Peak access road. (If you take the alternate route and go in the same direction you were just going, it will curve around and come to a T intersection. To continue to Simi Peak, turn right at this intersection. To go to the Dead Cow Trail connector, turn left.)

Continuing on the main Palo Comado Canyon Trail, you come to another T at 4.0 miles. A left turn will take you back past the old corral and down into Palo Comado Canyon. To the right is the connector for Dead Cow Trail. Proceed on this trail to 4.1 and a doubletrack on your right. For a great view of Oak Park and the Dead Cow Trail below, take this trail about 1 mile to the top of Simi Peak. It is very steep and rough in a couple of places, but the panorama is worth it.

Continuing on toward Dead Cow Trail at 4.1 miles (just past the Simi Peak Trail intersection), you come to a washed-out section of trail. Continue as best you can over to the other side and keep going up the doubletrack, curving to the right. (If you are riding in winter or spring and there has been a lot of rainfall, there will be a pond to your left. A narrow trail just a few yards past the washed-out section leads to the pond.)

At 4.5 miles, after climbing steeply up a double track, a trail comes in on the left. Affectionately referred to as Suicide, it leads to a ridiculously gnarly descent into the Oak Park trail system and Oak Canyon Regional Park. This is not recommended for anyone but the most advanced riders (or people who don't mind walking with their bikes).

Most riders elect to continue on the main trail. Directly ahead are two large barricades. Go past them; after the second one you reach the top of Dead Cow Trail, with Oak Park and King James Court below. Use caution since this is an extremely technical trail that can be deteriorated, loose, and tricky. Dead Cow Trail comes down to King James Court at about 5.8 miles. Turn left off the dirt, go 25 yards down to a gate, and head down King James to Lindero Canyon where you turn left. Go past a driveway on your right and to the next driveway, where there is a gap in the barricade (just over 6.0 miles). You are between King James and Wembley courts. Turn right off Lindero Canyon and continue down the singletrack to a small park and a paved pathway at 6.2 miles. Turn left on Bromely Street just a few yards down. Go across Bromely to the paved pathway (you are at the intersection of Bromely and Napoleon). Approximately 30 yards past the entrance to the paved pathway is a dirt path on the right that leads down into a fun canyon and into Oak Canyon Regional Park. You can also stay on the paved path which will lead you directly into Oak Canyon, but the goal here is to ride as much dirt as possible! At 6.6 miles you come to a T intersection with a trail coming in from the left. If you go straight, it takes you all the way out to Kanan Road. Instead, turn left and ride uphill to the rear of Oak Canyon Regional Park, over the sidewalk, and onto the access street. Turn right and continue down the street past parking on the right.

At this point you have a choice. You can ride pavement back to the car at the Doubletree/Sunnycrest curve, or continue on dirt (see below). To ride the pavement instead of the Oak Park trails back to your car, ride all the way out of Oak Canyon Regional Park on the access street. Exit onto Holly Tree (Kanan Road is the big street to the right), turning left after 0.6 mile to Doubletree. Go left again and ride 1.5 miles back to your car. Total mileage with this option is about 8.4 miles.

To continue on Oak Park dirt trails: Just past 6.8, miles you come to a driveway and house on the left. Looking up to the left you can see a trail cutting across a small ridge back up toward the hills. Turn into the driveway and go straight (not toward the house), looking for a cement drainage culvert. Cross over the culvert and follow the foot path to a connector. Turn left and ride up to a T intersection at just short of 7.0 miles. You will be looking down onto some red-tiled condominiums straight ahead.

Turn left up the hill and over a couple of roller hills. At 7.3 miles you come to another T. To the left is the Suicide trail from China Flat and another trail that leads back down to Oak Canyon. Turn right to continue on the loop route. At this point the trail becomes very steep and technical, with a lot of pushing and maybe even some carrying.

After rolling along some technical singletrack, you come to a Y at 7.9 miles. Bear uphill and to the left. (If you are losing daylight or just need to exit the trail system, you can turn right here and make your way downhill to Doubletree Drive.) Continuing on the singletrack from 7.9 miles, the trail dips and rolls along the hillside. At approximately 8.4 miles, look down and to your right — you should see a water tank and a wide dirt road. You can drop down to the right to this road (it may or may not be heavily rutted) and continue east to the base of the large knob hill that has the 4WD track going up its face, but the singletrack to the left is much more fun and is actually more direct. The knob hill is where you end up anyway by following the singletrack.

At 8.5 miles the singletrack pops out at a slightly wider access road that dead- ends to the left quickly. Turn right off the singletrack and continue down until the trail hooks into a jeep track and small saddle (8.6 miles). Turn left and go straight up the knob hill's four-wheel-drive track. This requires pushing most of the way. After reaching the summit of the knob hill (8.8 miles), continue along the ridge and some fun, fast, rolling hills. Down below you to your left is Palo Comado Canyon. At mile 9.4 you intersect with the Public Recreational Trail from Oak Park, where you turn right and descend to your car.

Paramount Ranch western town, Santa Monica Mountains National Recreation Area.

Mark Langton

PARAMOUNT RANCH

Access: The park is on Cornell Road in Agoura Hills. Take Freeway 101 to Kanan-Dume Road, go west (toward beaches) about half a mile to Cornell Road and turn left. (From Pacific Coast Highway you will have to travel almost all the way through the mountains via Kanan-Dume Road. Cornell is on the right just before you come to Agoura Road and Freeway 101.) Turn onto Cornell and continue to the Paramount Ranch entrance on the righthand side. Parking is to the left once you go down the driveway.

Continue on Cornell past Mulholland where it turns into Lake Vista. Stay on Lake Vista as it curves around Malibu Lake to Crags. Turn left on Crags and follow to the end and a locked park entrance gate. From Kanan-Dume Road, you can also get to the Crags Drive entrance to Malibu Creek State Park.

Paramount Ranch and the newly acquired Phase II property was once the site of the Renaissance Pleasure Faire. The quaint western town is a replica of an Old West town and is a working set for television and movie productions, including the popular "Dr. Quinn, Medicine Woman" television series. The park is frequently used for bluegrass banjo and fiddle concerts as well as special arts and crafts fairs and other events. It is an excellent place to visit with your family for picnicking or easy riding around the main western town. There is also more rugged riding in the property north of the park, and a short but fun singletrack trail goes along the perimeter of the park next to Mulholland Highway. *This is a heavily used equestrian area, so please use caution!*

Paramount Perimeter Trail

Mileage: 2.1 miles.
Level of Difficulty: Easy, with a couple of short, moderate-to-difficult sections.

From the parking lot in front of the town entrance, take the trail marked with a *"no car"* sign to the left of the paved parking area with the oak tree in the middle (you will be heading toward Cornell Road and away from the western town). The trail takes you past a park ranger residence on the left. At about 0.3 mile you come to a horse walkover at Mulholland and Cornell. Turn right down the narrow trail inside and along the fence to a short climb. You come to a Y; you can go to the right and up a short climb that leads back down to the trail you were just on, or keep straight and continue to a doubletrack that leads you back to the main creek trail at mile 0.7. Here you can go left and over to the Malibu Lake inlet and an exit road that puts you onto Mulholland Highway, or go right to the main parking and the western town at about mile 0.9. Continue through the parking lot on the paved road you came in on to the main driveway and fence at just past mile 1.0. Turn right on the trail inside the fence line, continue up toward Cornell, then follow along rolling hills to a left turn at mile 1.6. If you go straight you will end up in a large graded area. Left takes you back toward the parking lot and the western town.

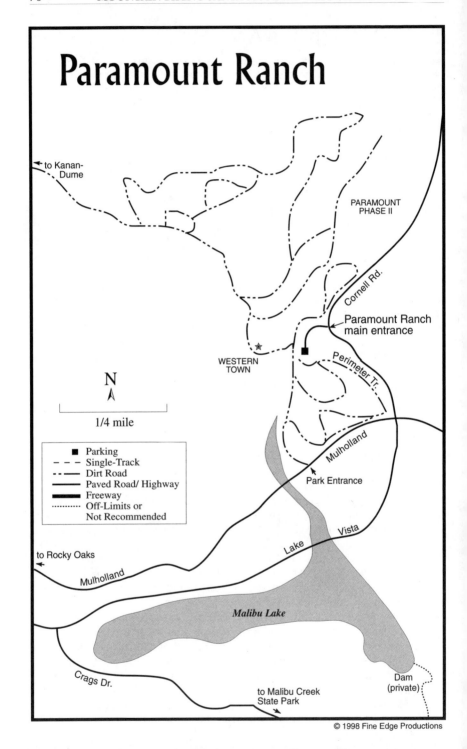

Paramount Ranch

to Kanan-Dume

PARAMOUNT PHASE II

Cornell Rd.

Paramount Ranch main entrance

WESTERN TOWN

Perimeter Tr.

N

1/4 mile

■ Parking
– – – Single-Track
–·–·– Dirt Road
——— Paved Road/ Highway
▅▅▅ Freeway
·········· Off-Limits or
        Not Recommended

Mulholland

Park Entrance

Vista

to Rocky Oaks

Lake

Mulholland

Malibu Lake

Crags Dr.

Dam (private)

to Malibu Creek State Park

© 1998 Fine Edge Productions

Phase II Trails

Mileage: Varies; the long loop is 5.6 miles with 3.1 miles of pavement.
Level of Difficulty: Easy to difficult.

At the time of this guide's printing, the trail plan for Paramount Ranch Phase II property had not yet been determined. The area adjacent to the western town is laced with dirt roads and roads that have deteriorated into singletrack. You may ride any of these short, fun roads and trails. Beware that there is private property to the north; please do not trespass. The most adventurous trail is one that goes out the back of the western town, the best way to access the trail network at the front part of the Phase II property.

From the western town, set your odometer at 0.0 and take the road between a grass field and a large barn around back of the town to a banked asphalt road. Take the road up and to the left. After it turns to dirt, continue to a Y at mile 0.6. To the right there is a short descent and steep climb that takes you over to short, criss-crossing doubletrack trails. Going left takes you past a second Y onto a rough, steep doubletrack that leads all the way over to Kanan-Dume Road 0.3 mile above Trout-dale Drive. At mile 1.3, after climbing a rock-strewn, rutted hill, you come to a saddle where you can look down and see Kanan-Dume Road and a beautiful view of the mountains to the northwest, and where Trout-dale Drive meets Kanan-Dume. Continue to mile 1.5, where the trail takes a sharp left and continues steeply down another 0.75 mile to Kanan-Dume Road. Once you are at Kanan-Dume, you can either turn around and climb back up the hill and descend back to Paramount Ranch, or take Kanan-Dume down to Troutdale Drive. You leave park property just before reaching the embankment that supports Kanan-Dume. As of this printing, the property here is under development and did not have a defined property line or access/egress. So please use discretion if you travel on this dirt road all the way over to Troutdale.

To continue back to Paramount Ranch via a loop on pavement, the easiest way is to climb up the embankment to Kanan-Dume. If you go left at the bottom of the descent you just came down, you will travel on a doubletrack to a fence and private property. Once on Kanan-Dume (be careful of traffic), go 0.3 mile to Troutdale Drive and turn left to Mul-holland Highway, mile 0.7. Turn left on Mulholland and continue 2 miles. As you approach mile 2.4 you see a bridge. On the other side of the bridge on the left is a locked gate and an entrance to Paramount Ranch. Follow downhill, turn right at the bottom, and continue back to the parking lot, or stay on Mulholland to the intersection of Mulholland and Cornell. Enter NPS property through the horse walkover and continue straight back to the parking area.

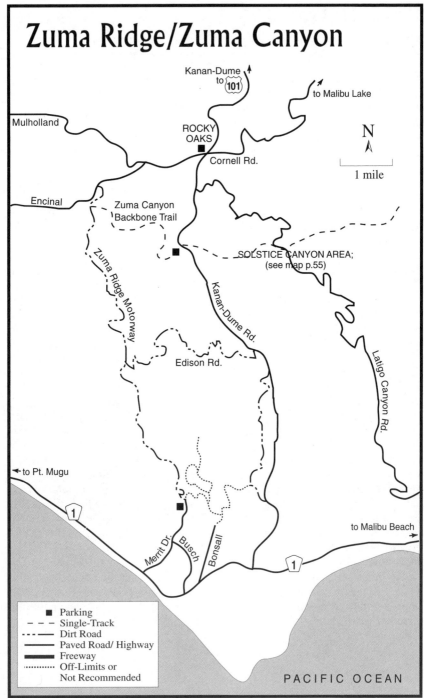

Zuma Ridge/Zuma Canyon

Kanan-Dume
to (101)

to Malibu Lake

Mulholland

ROCKY
OAKS

Cornell Rd.

N

1 mile

Encinal

Zuma Canyon
Backbone Trail

SOLSTICE CANYON AREA;
(see map p.55)

Zuma Ridge Motorway

Kanan-Dume Rd.

Edison Rd.

Latigo Canyon Rd.

◄ to Pt. Mugu

1

to Malibu Beach

Merrit Dr.   Busch   Bonsall

1

Legend

- ■ Parking
- – – – Single-Track
- ---- Dirt Road
- ——— Paved Road/ Highway
- ▬▬▬ Freeway
- ········ Off-Limits or
  Not Recommended

PACIFIC OCEAN

© 1998 Fine Edge Productions

CHAPTER 5

Kanan-Dume to Point Mugu

Zuma Canyon; Rocky Oaks National Recreation Area; Charmlee Natural Area County Park; Circle X Ranch

Kanan-Dume Road connects Freeway 101 with the beach at Point Dume and Zuma County Beach at the west end of Malibu. To the east is Latigo Canyon and the fire roads coming off Castro Crest in National Recreation Area property. Although the coastal side of the mountains here is generally developed, there are some major public parks in this area where new trails have been built. Both Zuma Canyon and Circle X Ranch have magnificent geological formations and unusually lush coastal canyons. The southern ridges of Zuma and Charmlee provide continuous views of Santa Monica Bay, and moisture from coastal fog and rain creates dramatic wildflower displays in the spring. *This is also horse country, so use caution when riding in the area.*

ZUMA CANYON

Access: From the east, you can park off Kanan-Dume Road at a dirt parking area approximately 0.1 mile north of Pacific Coast Highway on the left. This provides access to a singletrack descent to Lower Zuma Canyon. At the time of this guide's printing, the NPS was still determining the trail use plan for existing trails in Lower Zuma Canyon. Please check with the ranger station at the end of Bonsall Drive for access details if no trail use signage is in place. From the north, park at the Encinal/Zuma Ridge Motorway at the sign *Buzzards Roost* on Encinal Canyon, approximately 0.7 mile west of the junction of Encinal Canyon and Mulholland. This provides access to Zuma Ridge Motorway and the Zuma

Canyon section of the Backbone Trail. From the south off Pacific Coast Highway, turn right 0.8 mile west of Kanan-Dume on Bonsall Drive. Go 1.1 miles to the dead end and park. This is the entrance to Zuma Canyon. From the west off Pacific Coast Highway, turn left 1.4 miles west of Kanan-Dume on Morning View. Make an immediate right on Merrit Drive and climb 1.2 miles to a parking area where the road turns to dirt. This is the beginning of the Zuma Ridge Motorway. *Note:* Pacific Coast Highway runs east-west on this stretch: the ocean is due south.

Zuma Ridge Motorway

Mileage: 12.4 miles out and back (more with an Edison Road loop).
Level of Difficulty: Difficult.

This fire road climbs from the north end of Merrit Drive to the spine of the Santa Monicas and then descends to Encinal Canyon south of Mulholland Drive. The Edison road, which crosses Zuma Ridge at mile 2.8, allows you to ride east to Kanan-Dume or west to Trancas Canyon. However, there is no public access into Trancas Canyon, so you will eventually have to come back up the way you came. If you face the water tower on Merrit Drive, the road to the right drops down to Lower Zuma Canyon, and the two roads in front of you climb the Zuma Ridge Motorway. The steep road in the center and the more gradual climb on the left both enter the motorway.

0.0 mile: Go left and begin a long gradual climb up the fire road. At mile 0.5 the steeper road joins in, and the road overlooks the ocean and Zuma Canyon. At 1.0 there is a plateau over-

Zuma Ridge Motorway, Santa Monica Mountains National Recreation Area.

Brian Hemsworth

looking canyons both east and west. At mile 1.4, firebreaks go off to the right and dead-end shortly. At 2.8 the road crests and the Edison road crosses both east and west. The road climbs to a pinnacle at 4.2 miles and forks at 4.3, with the right fork going to a private ranch. Take the left turn for a steep descent to Encinal Canyon west of Camp Kilpatrick, ending at mile 6.2. Return the same way you came. The entrance to the Zuma Canyon section of the Backbone Trail is 0.7 mile from Encinal Canyon.

Edison Road into Zuma Canyon

Mileage: 13.1-mile loop from the south side of Zuma Ridge.
Level of Difficulty: Very difficult.
Access: Edison road crosses Zuma Ridge Motorway at mile 2.8 from the south or about 3 miles from the north at Encinal Canyon.

At Zuma Ridge Motorway and Edison Road, set your odometer at 0.0 mile. Turn east down a very steep, rocky 2-mile descent. It bottoms-out in lush, sycamore-studded, grassy canyon bottomland. After crossing a stream, you begin a steep, strenuous 2-mile climb on a loose, rocky road. At mile 4.3 there is a junction with a dead-end road to an electric tower on the left; continue on the main road. Begin the descent toward Kanan-Dume. At mile 4.9 bear left at the fork (right goes to a dead end at some concrete drain pipes). Edison Road connects with Kanan-Dume at mile 5.2. Obscured from the north by a hill, the entrance is located near a 50-mph speed limit sign and another sign indicating caution to descending trucks.

Turn right (south) toward the ocean. A short distance down Kanan-Dume there is a fire road entrance on the right with a chain across it and a small National Park Service boundary sign. At the Y, 0.5 mile farther, bear left and climb for a short stretch before descending as you parallel Kanan-Dume. You can take this fire road down to the trails that lead into Zuma Canyon, or stay on Kanan-Dume to the clearing at mile 7.4 and the big white house on the right. You will have to skirt the property along the fence to get onto the doubletrack that leads to the trail into Zuma Canyon. Follow this doubletrack to the north.

At 8.0 miles, turn left on a singletrack (right is the parallel Edison Road back to Kanan-Dume). This is a long, lovely descent into lower Zuma Canyon. *Caution: There could be a horse around every blind corner, especially on weekends.* At mile 9.5 connect with the main trail through lower Zuma Canyon and turn left. (The right goes up the canyon bottom.) Just past mile 9.6, turn right on a doubletrack trail signed *Equestrian.* Follow the trail up to the left, along a barbed wire fence and out across a gate to the Zuma Ridge parking area at Merrit Drive (mile 10.3). Please check with the ranger station at the entrance to Zuma Canyon for access details before riding these trails or in Zuma Canyon.

Mark Langton

Cheeseboro Canyon offers easy-to-moderate riding in the first two miles from the parking lot.

ROCKY OAKS

Access: From Freeway 101, take Kanan-Dume Road west to Mulholland High-way, turn right, and find the park entrance on the right in about 200 yards. From Pacific Coast Highway, take Kanan-Dume Road west to Mulholland Highway and turn left. Park in the lot or on the dirt shoulder of Mulholland. Calamigos Picnic Ranch entrance is on the left. (Mulholland and Latigo from this side are also alternate entrances for the Newton and Brewster motorways up to Castro Crest. Approximately a half-mile west of Mulholland on Kanan-Dume is Latigo Canyon. To get to Newton Motorway from Mulholland, take Latigo approximately 4 miles to a dirt turnout with an arch gate on the left with "Hel-lacious Acres" on top. Park just up the road at the locked gate. To get to Brew-ster Motorway from Mulholland, take Mulholland east approximately one mile to the motorway entrance on the right.)

Rocky Oaks is a relatively small parcel of 198 acres. It was previously owned by the Brown family who lived and ranched on the site for about 30 years before selling to the Park Service. It is speculated that the area sustained Chumash Indian activity since there are abundant oak groves and a natural spring, and caves on the west side of the park.

Rocky Oaks consists of two main trails, the Loop Trail and the Creek Trail, as well as a short out-and-back trail that is somewhat technical. The area is a great place for beginning mountain bikers or a family picnic. Kids can ride most of the trails, since they are relatively smooth and flat. The upper Loop Trail provides some challenge, but it is not very long. There is also a pond in the middle of the property that contains water most of the year. *Caution! There are many horseback riders who live nearby and use this park frequently.*

Loop Trail/Creek Trail/Pond Trail

Mileage: Short loops of approximately 1.2 miles; one out-and-back of 0.4 mile.
Level of Difficulty: Easy to moderate.

From the information kiosk trailhead, set your odometer at 0.0. Take the trail 30 yards to a T. Go left for access to Loop, Creek and Pond trails, or go right for access to lower section of Pond and Glade trails, where there is a large stand of oaks. For best riding take the left, and just short of mile 0.2 there is an intersection with upper and lower trails to the right and another trail that heads left and back toward Mulholland. The upper right trail is the Loop Trail, the lower is the Pond Trail, and the left trail is the out-and-back Creek Trail. The Creek Trail continues to the park boundary and private property at 0.4 mile.

Continuing the upper Loop Trail, a spur trail comes in at the left at 0.4 mile (from parking lot without Creek Trail mileage). No bikes are allowed, but it is an easy hike to an overlook knob. Continue on the Loop Trail to a Y at 0.65 mile. To the left is the park boundary and a short climb to some horse trails (not very rideable) that

Are we having fun yet?

Jim Hasenauer

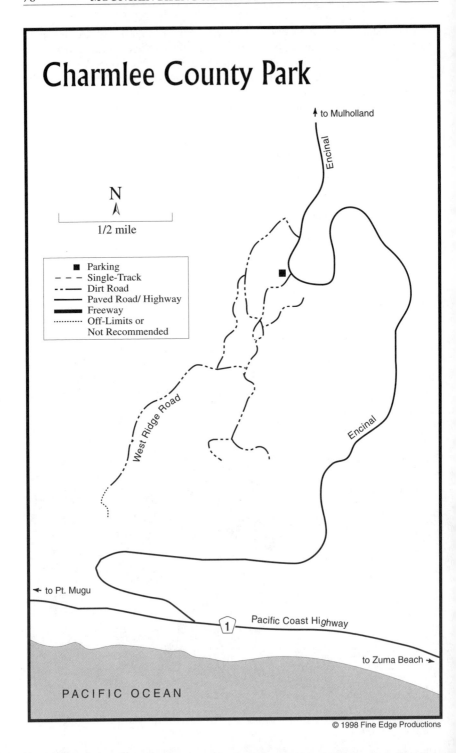

Charmlee County Park

lead back into the park. A right leads back down onto the floor of the park. At mile 0.9 you come to another Y; go right for the Pond Trail, and to the left for the Glade Trail and the large, shady oak grove with old farming equipment and a picnic table. Continue on the trail past the oaks back to more picnic tables and the parking lot, or turn right to get back to the Pond Trail. The total perimeter mileage of the Loop Trail is 1.2 miles.

CHARMLEE NATURAL AREA COUNTY PARK

Access: From Pacific Coast Highway, turn inland on Encinal Canyon (4 miles north of Kanan-Dume Road). The park entrance is on the left at 4.5 miles. If you're coming from Mulholland, head west across Kanan-Dume Road. At 0.6 mile bear left at the junction with Encinal Canyon Road. At 1.2 miles continue straight past the Zuma Ridge/Buzzards Roost fire road on your left. Encinal Canyon comes to a dead end after 4 miles. Turn left and proceed 2.3 miles to the Charmlee Natural Area entrance.

The 460-acre Charmlee Natural Area County Park was named for its last two private owners, Charmaine and Leonard Swartz. The property was part of an old Spanish land grant, and the many dirt roads here indicate a long history of ranching. The old ranch opened as a county park in 1981.

There is a nature center with a hillside display of the park's native plants, as well as many picnic sites and stunning views of the ocean. On a clear day, you can see from Catalina to the Channel Islands, with terrific views of the Santa Monicas. The park is famous for its wide variety of wildflowers.

Charmlee offers a variety of terrain and about 10 miles of rideable trails. Although it's a small park, there's a variation for every visit. There are some steep climbs and descents, but most of the riding is relatively flat, great for beginning mountain bicyclists. Be cautious, though, because the roads are very rutted and the park is often crowded with families. *Control your speed.*

Charmlee Trails

Mileage: Loops from 2 to 10 miles.
Level of Difficulty: Generally easy, but there is one difficult climb on West Ridge Road.

After parking, follow the main gravel road into the park. The nature center and restrooms are located on the right. Go through the gate to where the road turns to dirt.

0.0 mile: An oak-shaded picnic area is on the left. At about 0.3 mile there is a junction, and the left road goes through a meadow and inter-sects with several trails offering beautiful ocean views. Taking the right trail, you climb and then descend inland. There is another fork, with a right turn looping back to the parking area and Encinal Canyon. The left fork, West Ridge Road, descends sharply toward a park boundary at a water tower.

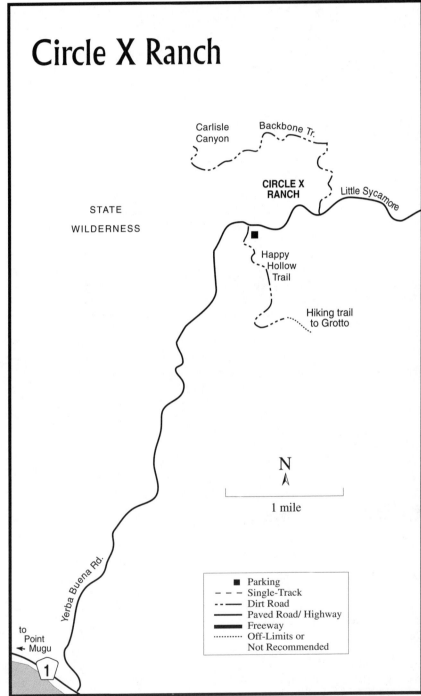

Circle X Ranch

Carlisle Canyon

Backbone Tr.

CIRCLE X RANCH

Little Sycamore

STATE

WILDERNESS

Happy Hollow Trail

Hiking trail to Grotto

N

1 mile

Yerba Buena Rd.

to Point
← Mugu

1

- ■ Parking
- – – – Single-Track
- –·–·– Dirt Road
- ——— Paved Road/ Highway
- ▬▬▬ Freeway
- ·········· Off-Limits or Not Recommended

CIRCLE X RANCH

Access: From Pacific Coast Highway, head inland at Yerba Buena Road. Climb 5 miles to the park headquarters on the right. Coming from Mulholland, turn west on Little Sycamore Canyon Road near the Decker and Lechusa junction. Little Sycamore Canyon Road becomes Yerba Buena Road. Pass the signed lot (equestrian parking) on the right at 4.8 miles and continue another mile to park headquarters.

Circle X was a former Boy Scout camp. There are individual and group campgrounds, two bunkhouses, a swimming pool (for campers only and you *must* bring your own certified lifeguard), an outdoor basketball court and many hiking trails. Some of these are open to bicycles. From park headquarters there is a short but beautiful ride or hike down to a grotto with a year-round stream and fantastic rock formations. From the upper parking lot, bicyclists may ride down into Carlisle Canyon and an old campground. This skirts California State Wilderness and the Mishe Mokwa Trail, currently *closed to bicycles.*

Happy Hollow Campground and the Grotto

Mileage: 3 miles out and back.
Level of Difficulty: Easy on Happy Hollow Road.
Note: Grotto Trail closed to bicycles.

0.0 mile: From the lower parking lot at park headquarters, descend a dirt road toward the campground. At 0.15 mile, bear right on Happy Hollow Road at the junction with the road to the group campground and Grotto Trail. Descend approximately one mile to Happy Hollow Campground and follow the stream bed to Grotto Trail. At about 1.5 miles, the stream bed becomes impassable to bikes. Hike and boulder-hop another 0.3 mile to the Grotto to see its pools and rugged rock formations. This is the headwaters of the Arroyo Sequit, which carries water from the mountains to the beach near Leo Carrillo State Park. Return the way you came.

Boney Mountain/Backbone Trail to Carlisle Canyon

Mileage: 5 miles out and back.
Level of Difficulty: Moderate to difficult.

0.0 mile: From the upper parking lot, 1 mile east of park headquarters on the left, enter the fire road and begin a very steep climb to the junction. The Mishe Mokwa singletrack is on the right at mile 0.25 *(closed to bikes).* Continue left on the fire road and begin a steady climb to mile 1.3, passing the Sandstone Peak trailhead on your left. This short singletrack, *closed to bikes*, climbs to the 3,111-foot summit of the tallest peak in the Santa Monicas. This is Sandstone Peak, also called Mt. Allen, which interestingly is composed of volcanic rock, not sandstone. Descend on the fire road to an abandoned campground in Carlisle Canyon. After the terrain flattens out you'll see the famous remains of the old Boy Scout outhouse at about 2.5 miles. The trails that connect with this point are *closed to bikes*, so you must return the way you came.

Jim Hasenauer likes to get dirty!

Mark Langton

CHAPTER 6

The Northern Santa Monicas

Westlake Open Space; Los Robles Canyon Open Space; Wildwood Park; North Ranch Open Space; Point Mugu State Park; Rancho Sierra Vista

The north end of the Santa Monica Mountains presents perhaps the most diverse and abundant riding opportunities of all the park regions in the Santa Monica Mountains National Recreation Area, including the Conejo Open Space Conservation Agency (COSCA) in Ventura County. COSCA property is maintained by the City of Thousand Oaks as an integral part of the lifestyle of the Conejo Valley, and in the case of the Los Robles Trail, it abuts National Park Service land at Rancho Sierra Vista.

Because of the differing use policies affecting state, national, and COSCA properties, please try to be aware of what land you are riding on and obey all rules. Local mountain bikers are fortunate to have access to the singletrack trails in COSCA, along with hikers and equestrians. Residents are proud and devoted to keeping COSCA suitable for multi-use recreation. The Conejo Open Space Trails Advisory Committee, a multi-use board made up of residents from the community, has been a remarkable model of establishing multi-use guidelines.

The Conejo Volunteer Patrol, a multi-use patrol modeled after the CORBA Mountain Bike Unit and equestrian Mounted Patrol Unit (NPS), is representative of the cooperative use of the area by hikers, equestrians, and cyclists. The patrol keeps a vigilant watch on COSCA property, as does a concerned and protective constituency of individuals. Both these groups are intolerant of reckless or irresponsible behavior, so it is of utmost importance that cyclists conduct themselves in the most careful manner possible. Ignoring prudent riding behavior could threaten the use pattern for cyclists in the future, as well as presenting a physical danger to other users. *Always control your speed and be watchful of other users around every turn!*

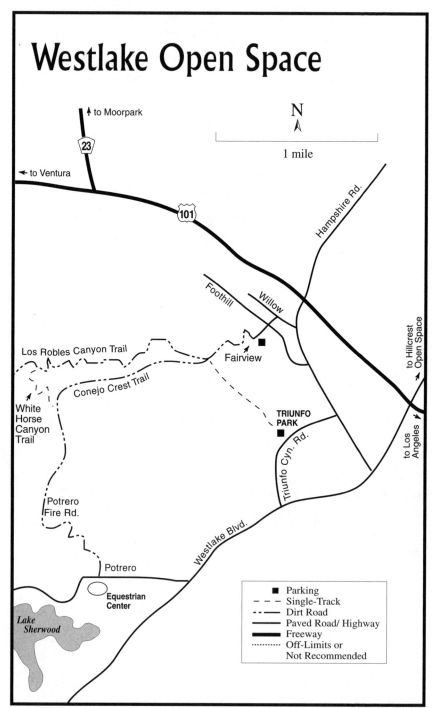

Westlake Open Space

to Moorpark

23

to Ventura

101

N

1 mile

Hampshire Rd.

Foothill

Willow

Los Robles Canyon Trail

Fairview

Conejo Crest Trail

White
Horse
Canyon
Trail

**TRIUNFO
PARK**

Triunfo Cyn. Rd.

to Hillcrest
Open Space

to Los
Angeles

Potrero
Fire Rd.

Potrero

Westlake Blvd.

Equestrian
Center

*Lake
Sherwood*

■ Parking
– – – Single-Track
–·–·– Dirt Road
——— Paved Road/ Highway
━━━ Freeway
·········· Off-Limits or
        Not Recommended

© 1998 Fine Edge Productions

Virtually all of COSCA property is rugged and steep, with only a few short, easy fire roads for riders of less than intermediate ability. There is a significant amount of challenging terrain in a relatively short distance, which makes the riding very strenuous yet rewarding. There are also several other areas in COSCA that can be accessed, but because they are interspersed in and around the Conejo Valley and must be connected by traveling streets and entering trailheads that are still not completely identified, we are including only the three major areas of COSCA: the Westlake Open Space/Los Robles Canyon Open Space, Wildwood Park, and North Ranch Open Space.

There are several species of native plants and flowers in Wildwood Park, some identified as rare and endangered by the California Native Plant Society and the Department of Fish and Game. For this reason, *stay on designated trails only.* Do not go off-trail, either by bike or on foot.

Wildwood Park, like so many other areas in the Santa Monicas and surrounding valleys, was home to Chumash Indian activity. The Cultural Center in Wildwood Canyon has many displays on the area's plant and animal populations, and offers interpretive outings. The park was established in 1966 and has been the site of many television and movie productions, including "Wuthering Heights," "The Shores of Iwo Jima," "The Rifleman," "Wagon Train," and "Gunsmoke." In fact, the Stagecoach Bluff Trail is so named because of the numerous buckboard dives staged from the cliffs. With the addition of Wildwood Mesa in 1987, there are now 1,700 acres of backcountry to enjoy. Again, it is imperative that you exercise caution and common sense when using this most delicately balanced area. Be advised that the park is very busy on weekends, especially in spring and fall, and on warm days in winter.

The soil composition in Wildwood Park requires more drainage after a rain, so don't be surprised if the park is closed to public use for as many as three days after a moderate or heavy rainstorm.

WESTLAKE OPEN SPACE

Access: There are several access points to the Westlake Open Space. From the east side you can enter at Fairview off the 101 at Hampshire, or across the street from the equestrian center off Potrero Road in Westlake Village. From the west, you can access the upper plateau before the Los Robles Ridge Trail by taking Moorpark Road off the 101, going south to Los Padres, left to Hillsborough, and right to top of the hill. Access is on the right. However, the majority of the trail network is off Hampshire to the east.

For Hampshire trail access, go north on Freeway 101 to Thousand Oaks, exit Hampshire Road, go south toward Westlake to Willow Lane (the first street after you go under the freeway from the San Fernando Valley/Agoura or after turning right off the freeway coming from Ventura). Turn right on Willow to Fairview Road, then left on Fairview. Fairview ends at Foothill Road. Straight ahead you see a dirt road going between some houses. You can drive up this road to a locked gate, but it is better to start riding here since the road is not well suited to vehicular travel.

Conejo Crest Loop, White Horse Canyon Trail, Triunfo Park Trail

Mileage: 6.8 miles, with shorter loops available.
Level of Difficulty: Moderate to difficult, with some advanced technical singletrack skills required.

At Foothill and Fairview, set your odometer to 0.0. Continue up the fire road to a pump house on the left and a locked gate at mile 0.3. Go over the gate and turn right on the fire road. At about 1 mile, you come to a three-way intersection. Straight ahead you can see the fire road as it dips down into a saddle and then reappears under a row of wire towers. Going left takes you back toward Westlake and houses; to the right is a steep climb that leads to a very technical singletrack that ends at Freeway 101 and Rancho Road. Continue straight, descending quickly and then climbing steeply to another intersection at mile 1.2. To the right you can see a fire road descent, which is the Los Robles Canyon Trail over to the

Los Robles Ridge Trail. Just behind you, back down the steep climb, is the entrance to Triunfo Park Trail. This is a very technical singletrack of 0.9 mile that goes down to Triunfo Park in Westlake. For the Conejo Crest and White Horse Canyon Trail, turn left uphill at this intersection onto the narrow, rocky doubletrack.

Continue climbing until the hill tops out at a T. Here you have a beautiful view of the Santa Monicas to the west. The road winding up behind the rocky knob hill across the valley is Decker Road. Down to the left you can see part of Westlake Lake, and above that and to the right is Westlake Reservoir. Go right from the T intersection to continue on Conejo Crest (left drops quickly to

Middle Los Robles Trail, with Thousand Oaks in background.

Mark Langton

Overlook Trail in Pt. Mugu State Park with Pacific Ocean in the background and the southern tip of the Channel Islands in the distance.

houses). You will be on a ridge trail that is known as The Cobbles because of the rocky surface of the trail. Just past mile 1.8, you come to a descent that is very steep and loose. *Please use caution.* At the bottom of the steep descent (mile 1.9) there is a trail to the right that takes you directly into White Horse Canyon. Continue straight on this fun, rolling doubletrack to mile 2.2 and a fire road T. Going right takes you into White Horse Canyon; left goes to the beginning of the White Horse Canyon Trail.

Continue to the left downhill and then up and over another rise. At 2.4 miles there is a sign on the right for the White Horse Canyon Loop. The Equestrian Alternative Trail to the left is a fun route down to the houses below. Continuing on the fire road straight ahead will take you to Potrero Road and the equestrian center.

Turn right onto the White Horse Canyon Trail for a short but extremely fun singletrack that takes you over to the main fire road at 2.7 miles into White Horse Canyon. Turn left downhill and follow to mile 3.4, and the main Los Robles Canyon fire road. From here, left takes you to the upper plateau and Hillsborough trailhead (and Los Robles Ridge Trail); right takes you back to where you came in off Fairview.

Continue right on the fire road to a fun descent and then a series of moderate switchback climbs. To your left is the Conejo Valley and Freeway 101. At 4.6 miles you arrive back at the three-way intersection and the entrance to Triunfo Park Trail. From here you can go back to where you started or descend Triunfo Park Trail.

If you choose to take the Triunfo Park Trail, you come to the end of the trail at a locked gate. To the left is a trail that takes you around the sand volleyball court toward a steep walk-up. Continuing uphill, it flattens out a bit and then gets very steep again. At the top of this second steep section you can turn left and follow the fire road up to the first three-way inter-section you came to when you began your ride. From this point, turn right and continue back down to the locked gate and pump house on your left (Fairview).

For a less strenuous loop, instead of following the fire road up after climbing the two steep sections, go left downhill about 50 yards from the knoll you're on and then turn right at the bottom onto a narrow double-track. Just a short way down is a motorcycle trail on the left going straight down into a small valley. On the other side you can see another fire road, the one you want. Go down the trail and up the other side of the valley to a trail that merges you into the fire road. Stay on the main fire road, bearing right past the first Y in about 50 yards, then left at anoth-er Y, mile 1.6. Continue to a locked gate and pump station (about 1.9 miles), then turn right to go back down to Fairview.

LOS ROBLES CANYON OPEN SPACE

Los Robles Canyon Open Space offers several miles of interconnected single-tracks and fire roads with a variety of terrain and vegetation. Because Los Rob-les is surrounded by residential areas, you never feel completely free of the city. You see houses, the freeway or construction almost everywhere you ride here. Still, the rides are challenging, and there are many wildflowers in season. *Cau-tion: The area is heavily used by equestrians, especially on weekends.* The main Los Robles Trail runs 10 miles west to east between Newbury Park and Westlake Vil-lage. (Hidden Valley and Rancho Sierra Vista are to the south.) There are sev-eral connectors coming in from the north and south along the way. At the east end, the main trail forks to three different trailheads: Fairview, Triunfo Park and Lake Sherwood. The trail description below goes from west to east, but you can ride it in either direction.

Los Robles Canyon and Los Robles Ridge Trail

Mileage: 10 miles one way.
Level of Difficulty: Moderate to difficult with some very difficult, technical singletrack sections.
Access: Parking lot on Potrero Road, 0.5 mile east of Wendy. There's water and trail informa-tion at the trailhead. Other access: Moorpark Road/Fairview Road/Triunfo Park/Lake Sherwood.

0.0 mile: Starting at the trail leading from the gravel parking lot, climb a short way to a driveway (private). Go straight across and follow the trail to the right. Just a few yards up the hill (0.2 mile), the trail veers left downhill to a singletrack on the right. Follow the trail as it dips and rolls, with resi-dential property below you. At 1.3 miles you come to the intersection

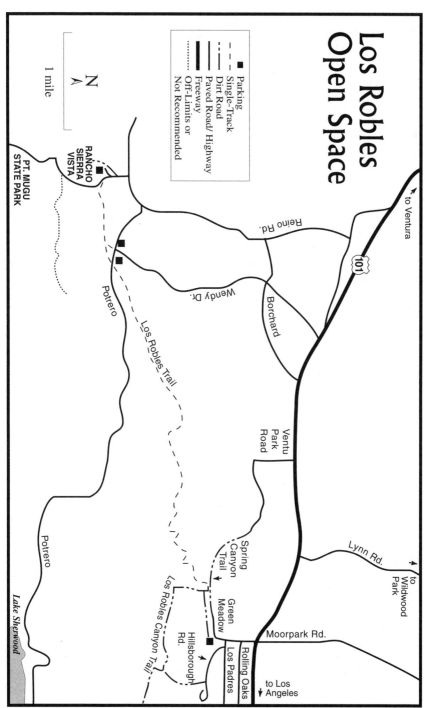

Los Robles Open Space

Legend:
- ■ Parking
- Single-Track
- Dirt Road
- Paved Road/ Highway
- Freeway
- Off-Limits or Not Recommended

N

1 mile

with Felton Street Trail coming in from the left. This leads to Felton Street and Lynn Road approximately 0.3 mile.

Continue up and to the right for the Los Robles Trail. There will be a series of steep climbs and descents along a double rail horse fence. At mile 2.0 turn left at the Y. At 2.2 turn left at the fork heading uphill. Do not go straight as it leads to private property. The trail will switchback several times and come to another intersection at mile 2.6. The left trail is the Rosewood Trail which leads to a great 1.8-mile descent that winds down to Lynn Road in Newbury Park, just west of Ventu Park Road. To your left (north) you will also see a picnic table with a great view of the Pacific Ocean. On a clear day you can see the Channel Islands.

Go right to continue on Los Robles Trail. At almost 2.8 miles you come to another intersection just below private property. Do not go onto private property. Bear left at the intersection to continue. At 3.1 miles you come to a wide dirt road which is a private driveway extension of Ventu Park Road. Do not go up or down this road. Go straight across to the singletrack trail on the other side. Climb the short steep hill and two switchbacks, and follow the contour of the mountain for approximately 1.5 miles. The trail then begins descending a mile-long section with a series of switchbacks. Be careful of other users coming uphill. Use extreme caution through this entire section. Control your speed and avoid skidding through the turns.

At mile 5.7, the trail intersects with Spring Canyon Trail; bear right and climb to a fork. Go right at the top of the hill, following signs to Lake

Sherwood and Triunfo Park (left goes to Moorpark Road). Climb the steep hill. At 6.3 miles, you pass a picnic table in an oak grove where you go left at a junction just past the sign: *Los Padres Road .5 miles, Fairview Road 4 miles, Lake Sherwood Road 4 miles.* Climb the steep hill, cross a dirt road and then go through the center of Upper Meadow (upper plateau). You come to an intersection with a gate on the right. To the left is Hillsborough Street, which leads down to Moorpark Road. Cross over the metal gate at mile 7.7. At 7.8 miles to the right is the White Horse Canyon Trail. To ride the rest of the Los Robles Trail, continue straight on the main fire road. (See Westlake Open Space trail descriptions for routes and distances in this area and from this point on Los Robles Trail.)

There are several options once you get to the Westlake Open Space. You can turn around and go back the same way, which in itself is a very different ride from the direction you just came. Many people take Potrero Road through Hidden Valley back to their cars in Newbury Park. If you choose to do this, turn right back at the White Horse Canyon Trail. If you make no turns off the main trail, you eventually come to Potrero Road and the equestrian center. (See White Horse Canyon and Conejo Crest trail descriptions.) Once you are on Potrero Road, turn right and continue all the way through Hidden Valley. You pass by cattle and horse ranches, then climb up out of the valley. The descent takes you a half-mile farther down to the entrance to Los Robles Ridge Trail on Potrero and the Wendy Walk-In.

You can also take Hampshire Road to Thousand Oaks Boulevard and sur-

Mark Langton

Overlook Trail in Pt. Mugu State Park with Pacific Ocean in the background and the southern tip of the Channel Islands in the distance.

face streets back to Newbury Park. Once you have exited Westlake Open Space at Fairview (see Westlake Open Space trail descriptions), turn left on Hampshire under Freeway 101 to Thousand Oaks Boulevard. Turn left, proceed to Moorpark Road, then turn right. Go up to Hillcrest Drive, turn left and follow all the way to intersection of Lynn and Hillcrest. The Oaks Mall will be on your left. Turn right on Hillcrest and continue until it runs into Camino Dos Rios. Turn left and continue over the freeway, with Camino Dos Rios turning into Wendy Drive. Follow Wendy back to Potrero and turn left; parking is located a half-mile up Potrero.

WILDWOOD PARK

Access: From Freeway 101, exit Lynn Road, travel east 3 miles to Avenida de los Arboles and turn left. Continue to end of Arboles to parking on the left (Arboles intersects Big Sky Drive). Park in the lot just off Arboles, or continue on a dirt road into the park, where there is another parking area in about a half-mile.

The parking lot at Arboles and Big Sky is the best place to begin all rides. There are several main rides originating from this parking lot, from short and easy to long and difficult. There is also proposed open space at the northern boundary past the water treatment plant north of Arroyo Conejo. At the time of this guide's printing there was no definite trail use plan, but the area is rideable.

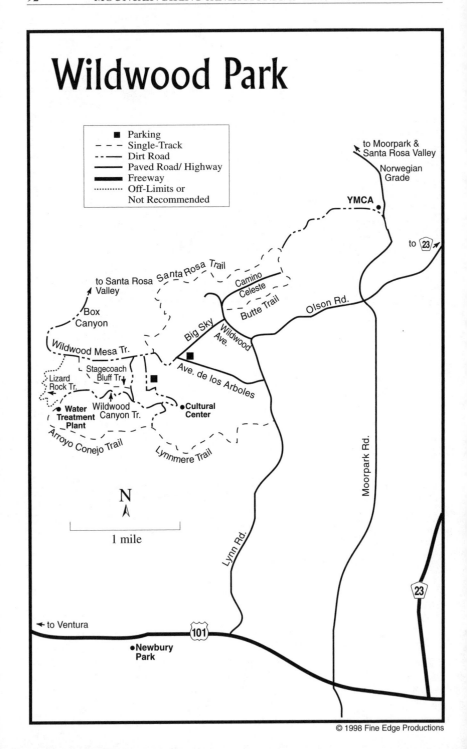

Wildwood Park

■ Parking
– – – Single-Track
-··-··- Dirt Road
———— Paved Road/ Highway
▬▬▬▬ Freeway
·············· Off-Limits or
        Not Recommended

to Moorpark &
Santa Rosa Valley

Norwegian
Grade

YMCA

to 23

Santa Rosa Trail

to Santa Rosa
Valley

Camino
Celeste

Box
Canyon

Butte Trail

Olson Rd.

Big Sky

Wildwood Ave.

Wildwood Mesa Tr.

Ave. de los Arboles

Lizard
Rock Tr.

Stagecoach
Bluff Tr.

Water
Treatment
Plant

Wildwood
Canyon Tr.

Cultural
Center

Arroyo Conejo Trail

Lynnmere Trail

Moorpark Rd.

N

1 mile

Lynn Rd.

23

to Ventura

101

Newbury
Park

© 1998 Fine Edge Productions

Wildwood Mesa Trail, Stagecoach Bluff Trail, Lizard Rock Trail

Mileage: 2.5 miles (6.3 with Lizard Rock Trail, not recommended for bikes).
Level of Difficulty: Easy to difficult; some technical singletrack skills are required.

From the parking lot at Arboles, set your odometer to 0.0 and take the road to the left into Wildwood Park. Continue to a locked gate, go around the gate and go straight. Wildwood Mesa Trail rolls gently, with two main access roads into Wildwood Canyon on the left (south), one of which leads to the inside parking lot. Continue on the mesa to a Y at mile 0.9. Going right takes you down into Box Canyon, the Santa Rosa Valley, and the Lizard Rock Trail.

If you take the right at the Y, you come to the cutoff for Box Canyon and Lizard Rock Trail on the right at 0.06. Descend the Box Canyon Trail about a half-mile *(watch for horses coming up)* to Lizard Rock Trail on the left. This is actually a well-used game trail and is not maintained. It is steep, narrow, and not recommended for bikes in either direction. It's mostly hike-a-bike up to Lizard Rock.

For an alternate route, from the Y at mile 0.9 on the Mesa Trail, go left another tenth of a mile to the Stagecoach Bluff Trail on the left. The trail becomes singletrack, rolling for a while and then climbing to the rocky bluffs. Continuing along the bluff, the trail is rocky and technical for a short stretch, and then drops to the left toward the mesa, becoming even more technical. Follow the trail and bear left until it meets an access road. From here you can go down into Wildwood Canyon or back to the parking lot on Arboles.

Wildwood Canyon Loop via Lizard Rock

Mileage: 4.4 miles.
Level of Difficulty: Moderate to difficult, with a steep rocky descent recommended for advanced riders only.

Take Wildwood Mesa Trail toward Stagecoach Bluff Trail (see previous directions). Continue past Stagecoach Bluff Trail up the steep hill to a trail on the left at 1.3 miles signed: *To lower Wildwood Canyon.* To the north is the entrance to the proposed open space, and directly below you can see (and possibly smell) the water treatment plant. The trail down into lower Wildwood Canyon is very steep, with loose rocky terrain and several steep, tight switchbacks near the bottom. On warm days when the wind is blowing east out of the canyon the water treatment plant's aroma can literally make it hard to breathe as you descend into the canyon. At the bottom of the trail into lower Wildwood Canyon, turn left to go back up Wildwood Canyon and past the waterfall. (A right at the bottom heads to Arroyo Conejo and the proposed open space.)

Turn left and follow the single-track trail 0.2 mile to where it intersects with a wider trail and turn left. You cross a stream, then come to another Y in 0.13 mile. Veer right toward the oak grove and picnic tables. (The steep hill on the left goes up past the Teepee and to the Mesa Trail.) Cross another stream and head left up canyon past Sycamore Flats. You come to a picnic area another half-mile up the trail with a waterfall on the right. Take the trail to the left, continue to the steps where the chain link fence begins, and follow the trail along the fence.

At mile 2.2 you come to an intersection. The steep trail to the left leads up to the Teepee. The wide, flat dirt road straight ahead leads to the cultural center and fire road that switches back up to the inside parking lot and Mesa Trail. The route to the right and down leads to a creek crossing and long steep climb up to the Lynnmere Trail. (At 0.5 mile up the hill the Lynnmere Trail crosses the fire road, heading east to Lynn Road, or west along the ridge line, then below some houses, and eventually down into Arroyo Conejo and the water treatment plant.) To continue back to Arboles and Big Sky, go straight toward the cultural center and follow the fire road up into the parking lot and to Mesa Trail.

Lynnmere Trail from Lower Wildwood Canyon through Arroyo Conejo

Mileage: 4.4 miles from water treatment plant.
Level of Difficulty: Moderate to difficult, with some technical singletrack skills required.

You can access Arroyo Conejo by either going down Wildwood Canyon from the inside parking lot or taking the Mesa Trail over to the steep trail leading down to Lower Wildwood Canyon (see previous directions). Taking the Wildwood Canyon route, go through the inside parking lot down to the intersection below the Teepee fire road, where you set your odometer to 0.0. Following the Wildwood Canyon Trail down canyon, you pass the waterfall, cross a stream, and then reach a second stream crossing. Go straight ahead to yet another stream crossing to the left. Continue to a trail on the right signed *Lizard Rock Trail (right), Skunk Hollow Picnic Area (left)*. Go right and continue on the trail past the water treatment plant to a paved drive. Continue on the drive 0.2 mile to a bridge crossing on the left. Once you are on the other side of the water treatment plant, bear left to a stream crossing in another 0.15 mile.

Continue up Arroyo Conejo, staying on the main trail (stream bed). There are several stream crossings. At 1.3 miles you come to a steep hill on the left that climbs up to houses. At 1.8 the hill tops out. Bear left across the cement drainage culvert onto the singletrack that skirts to the left of the houses. Continue on this trail to an intersection at 2.5 miles. Turn right up a rocky hill and continue on the trail until you get to the fire road that leads up from Wildwood Canyon, 3.3 miles. From here you can continue on the Lynnmere Trail over to Lynn Road, or descend the fire road to the intersection below Teepee fire road. If you continue on the Lynnmere Trail, stay on the trail, taking no off-shoot trails. Once you get to Lynn, turn left to Arboles, then left again to the parking lot.

Lynnmere Trail Loop from Arboles Parking Lot to Wildwood Canyon

Mileage: 3.5 miles.
Level of Difficulty: Moderate to difficult, with some technical singletrack skills required.

This is the preferred direction of travel for this section of Lynnmere Trail. From Arboles parking lot, go back out toward Lynn Road and turn right on Lynn. At mile 1.3 on Lynn you will come to the entrance to Lynnmere Trail at a fence on the right, just after Avenida de los Flores. Follow the trail to the north into the park. At mile 1.6 the trail veers left down an embankment. Bear to the left as you approach the bottom, and the trail leads you to a stream crossing. After crossing the stream, take the left trail. At about 2.0 miles, after a steep, rutted descent, you come to a Y. Take a right for a rideable trail. Continue to 3.0 miles and the main fire road from Wildwood Canyon. You can descend to the Teepee intersection or go up the fire road 25 yards and to the right to continue on Lynnmere Trail to Arroyo Conejo and the water treatment plant.

Butte Trail/Santa Rosa Trail Loop

Mileage: About 4 miles.
Level of Difficulty: Moderate to difficult, with some advanced singletrack skills required.

The Butte and Santa Rosa trails wrap up, around and over Mountcleff Ridge. Santa Rosa Trail is one of the most enjoyable, and technical, singletrack trails in Wildwood. *Please use caution as this trail is frequented by both hikers and equestrians every day of the week.*

This trail can be ridden in both directions, but for maximum enjoyment you will need to ride on pavement to get to the far end so you can descend the Santa Rosa Switchbacks, a set of ten tight, rocky switchbacks that will test the best technical riders. From the Arboles parking lot, take Big Sky Drive and follow to Wildwood Avenue, 0.65 mile; turn left. Continue on Wildwood Avenue just under 0.2 mile to the entrance of Butte Trail on the right at mile 0.8. This narrow singletrack trail climbs steeply up over a saddle of volcanic rock, then descends a wide singletrack to a jeep road at mile 1.5. Turn left on a doubletrack and continue on the trail with houses on the left.

At 1.7 miles you see on your left the end of Camino Celeste (which you can also take from Wildwood Avenue to access the Santa Rosa Trail via pavement). Continue straight over a dirt road and past a locked gate on the left. Go up a short hill and continue downhill to Santa Rosa Trail on the left at mile 1.8. Follow Santa Rosa Trail, with Santa Rosa Valley below you. Along the trail you pass luxury homes that were built in the late 1980s. At 3.26 miles you cross over Mountcleff Ridge from the Santa Rosa Valley side to the Wildwood Mesa side. Below you is the parking lot at Arboles and Big Sky. This is the beginning of the Santa Rosa Switchbacks. Stay on this trail until it intersects with the Wildwood Mesa Trail at just under 4.0 miles. From here you can continue on the Mesa Trail to Stagecoach Bluff, ride down into Wildwood Canyon, or head over to Lynnmere Trail (see previous descriptions).

NORTH RANCH OPEN SPACE

Access: Since the North Ranch Open Space Trail originates at two trailheads (Sandstone Hills Trail and Hillcrest Open Space Preserve), there are two distinct starting points. Both directions are enjoyable, but for optimum enjoyment it is recommended to begin at the southeastern trailhead in Oak Park—Sandstone Hills Trail. Directions and mileage given here start from this trailhead. From the 101 Ventura Freeway, exit Lindero Canyon Road and travel east 2.8 miles to the corner of Kanan and Lindero Canyon roads.

There are several starting points. The first is on the northeast corner (upper left), which puts you on a rolling access road through open fields, paralleling Lindero Canyon Road. There is no real parking at this location, and the area may be developed in the future. The second starting point is accessed by turning left onto Kanan Road from Lindero Canyon Road and going to the first right, Falling Star. Go approximately a quarter mile on Falling Star, and on the right is a barricade and parking along the street. Head toward Lindero Canyon Road on the doubletrack; when you intersect with a dirt road (the one that originates at the corner of Lindero Canyon Road and Kanan Road), turn left toward the mountains. Follow this road as it takes you behind some houses and up to Pathfinder

Installing a sign on the Rosewood Trail (Los Robles Open Space) in COSCA, with Thousand Oaks in the background.

Mark Langton

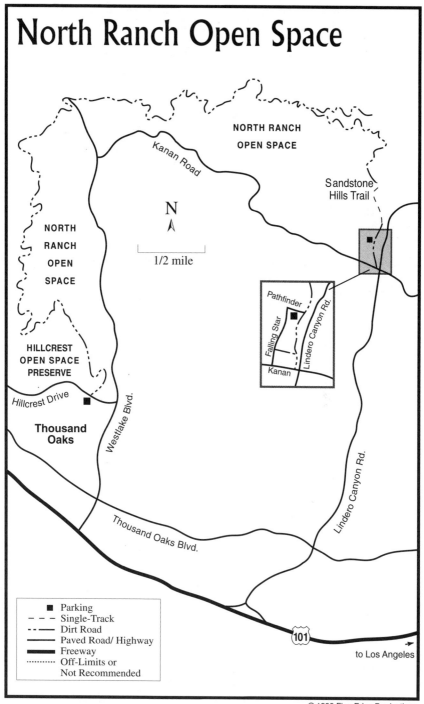

North Ranch Open Space

NORTH RANCH OPEN SPACE

Kanan Road

Sandstone Hills Trail

N

1/2 mile

NORTH RANCH OPEN SPACE

Pathfinder

Falling Star

Lindero Canyon Rd.

Kanan

HILLCREST OPEN SPACE PRESERVE

Hillcrest Drive

Thousand Oaks

Westlake Blvd.

Lindero Canyon Rd.

Thousand Oaks Blvd.

101

to Los Angeles

■ Parking
– – – Single-Track
–·–· Dirt Road
——— Paved Road/ Highway
▬▬▬ Freeway
·········· Off-Limits or Not Recommended

© 1998 Fine Edge Productions

Street. Cross over Pathfinder Street and continue up the Sandstone Hills Trail.

The third starting point is accessed directly off Pathfinder Street onto the Sandstone Hills Trail. Pathfinder Street is 0.3 mile from Kanan Road. Turn right on Pathfinder Street from Falling Star and go just a few yards to the top of the hill. The Sandstone Hills Trail access is on your left.

The North Ranch Open Space Trail offers a bit of singletrack and some challenging fire road riding. It also takes you up to the base of some rocky peaks and caves that are fun for exploring and looking out from onto the cities of Westlake Village and Oak Park, and northern Santa Monicas. Because of the close proximity of the trail to homes, please respect private property.

North Ranch Open Space Trail— Sandstone Hills Trail, Hillcrest Open Space Preserve

Mileage: 7.5 miles one way (8.7 with wire break extension).
Level of Difficulty: Mostly moderate with some difficult technical singletrack and steep fire road climbs and descents.

Mile 0.0: At the entrance to Sandstone Hills Trail, step over the barricade and climb a short hill, then continue down a dirt road with homes to your left. As the hill flattens out, look to the right to where you can see water bars and a singletrack trail. This is the most technical section in the North Ranch Open Space. Continue up the trail, dive down into a small arroyo, then climb steeply up some switchbacks. At 0.5 mile you come up behind more homes and past a fire tower. Continue straight ahead to the railroad tie steps. A little more technical riding and then this singletrack dumps you onto a fire road, where you go right (uphill). At 0.75 mile you come to a chain link fence. Continue past the fence and along the fire road, which is generally rolling and moderately difficult.

At mile 1.4 you come to a wire break road that takes you to some caves and a good viewpoint. The total mileage of the wire break road up and back is 1.2 miles (0.6 mile one way), giving you the opportunity to add a nice overlook and fun descent to your ride. Right before you get to the end of the wire break there is a foot path to your left that leads to the rock formations and caves above. From here you can see from Topanga Canyon to Castro Crest to Boney Mountain in the Boney State Wilderness near Point Mugu. On a clear day you can make out the Pacific Ocean to the west and the Channel Islands off the coast of Santa Barbara.

Continuing on the main North Ranch Open Space Trail, at 1.5 miles you come to an intersection where you bear right. From here you can see several trails below that branch off the main trail to the left, toward Kanan Road, which at this point parallels the North Ranch Open Space Trail. Once you descend the steep hill just ahead, you can explore these trails, some of which are fun motocross-type trails. While some of them loop back toward the main trail, most lead down toward Kanan Road and into private homes with no outlet. However, if you're losing daylight or are in need of getting out quickly, these roads and trails can give you access to Kanan Road rather than having to go all the way to Westlake Boulevard to the north.

This section of the trail is fun and fast, dropping you into a small meadow (2.2 miles). Continue on the dirt road to a Y at 2.3 miles and bear right (the left fork is a main access to Kanan Road). Just a tenth of a mile ahead is another intersection (2.4 miles). Continue straight through and begin climbing. Below and to the right is the Albertson Motorway which is off limits to bikes. At 2.8 miles you come to another Y; bear left uphill and continue along another fun rolling section that leads to a paved driveway with a water tank on the right (3.3 miles). Go left and either get onto the wide driveway or go onto the small dirt trail to the left of the driveway.

The dirt takes you over to the driveway a little farther up. At the time of printing there were no homes in the area, so the outlet may change. This is another reason to start from Pathfinder Street, since the trail access at this point may be different. Continue on the driveway and follow it to Westlake Boulevard (entrance to Lange Ranch, a major four-lane street) at 3.9 miles.

Continue across Westlake Boulevard to the barricade and COSCA boundary marker. This is the Hillcrest Open Space Preserve. Follow this wide dirt road just a short way to a lefthand turn at 4.0 miles that goes steeply up hill. This leads shortly up to a Y at 4.1 miles, where you bear right. (Bearing left will take you up a really steep hill and over to a four-wheel-drive trail that follows the ridge over to Hillcrest Drive. It has several extremely steep climbs and descents that are not much fun.)

At 4.5 miles you come to an intersection and a housing development

Wood Canyon Vista Trail in Point Mugu State Park.

Mark Langton

straight ahead. Take the left fire road with the white, chalky dirt. It rolls along the contour of the ridge, rising and dropping all the way to Hillcrest Drive. At mile 5.9 you ascend a rise and come up to a spot where a trail drops away to your right. The canyon below is in a development zone and is not recommended for access. To the left is a four-wheel-drive track up to the ridge. Looking down toward the 101 Freeway you can see a large structure, the Thousand Oaks Civic Arts Plaza, which houses City Hall and a large performing arts center. Continue on the fire road almost to 6.5 miles and a T intersection. Go left uphill to another T intersection at 6.7 miles. (To the left you can see the four-wheel-drive trail that leads back toward Westlake Boulevard. This is a

great place to view hawks catching rides on the thermals that rise from the canyon.) Turn right for your final descent to Hillcrest Drive at 7.5 miles.

From here you can either ride the trail back to the Sandstone Hills Trail and Pathfinder Street where you parked, or ride the road back for a scenic trip past many opulent houses. The directions and mileage for the road route is as follows: Leave the dirt and turn left on Hillcrest Drive to Westlake Boulevard, turn left, go to Kanan Road (2.2 miles from Hillcrest Drive), turn right and continue 2.5 miles to Falling Star. Turn left on Falling Star and right on Pathfinder Street; hopefully your car will be waiting for you. Total mileage using this road route is 12.75 miles.

POINT MUGU STATE PARK

Access: From the beach at Sycamore Canyon Campground, 5 miles north of Leo Carrillo State Beach on Pacific Coast Highway. A $5 entry fee is required for campground day use. If you're coming from Newbury Park or Ventura, take 101 Freeway and exit on Wendy Drive, turning left (south) toward the mountains. In 3.2 miles, Wendy ends at Potrero Road. Turn right. At the junction with Reino, bear left on Potrero Road, then turn left on Pinehill (at the stop sign) onto a dirt road. Follow the dirt road to the parking lot. (This is the current entrance. However, by mid-1999 a new entrance, including a cultural center, will be located off Potrero Road across from the Dos Vientos development. To get to this entrance from the 101 Freeway: exit Wendy Drive, go south (toward the beach) to Lynn Road. Turn right on Lynn to Reino Road, where Lynn becomes Potrero. Continue on Potrero 1.5 miles to park entrance on the left. From this parking lot, trail mileage will increase by approximately half a mile.) Ride your bike around the locked fire gate to enter the park.

Point Mugu State Park is one of the most popular bicycling areas in the Santa Monicas. It has spectacular scenery and several loop options for bicyclists.

The main trail—actually an old fire road—is relatively flat and connects Newbury Park with the beach, where there is car camping at Sycamore Canyon Campground.

The park offers five miles of ocean shoreline, two long rides in canyon bottomland, and a long ridge ride overlooking both the canyon and ocean. La Jolla

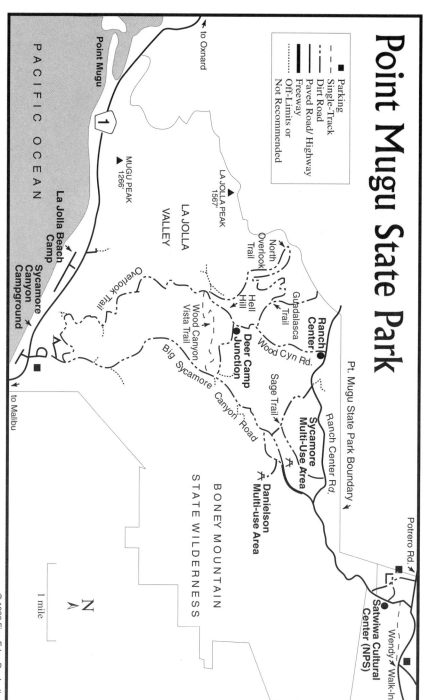

Point Mugu State Park

- ■ Parking
- – – – Single-Track
- – · – · Dirt Road
- ——— Paved Road/ Highway
- ——— Freeway
- · · · · · · Off-Limits or Not Recommended

PACIFIC OCEAN

Point Mugu

to Oxnard

LA JOLLA PEAK 1567'

▲ MUGU PEAK 1266'

LA JOLLA VALLEY

La Jolla Beach Camp

Sycamore Canyon Campground

North Overlook Trail

Overlook Trail

Hell Hill

Wood Canyon, Vista Trail

Deer Camp Junction

Guadalasca Trail

Ranch Center

Wood Cyn Rd.

Big Sycamore Canyon Road

Sage Trail

to Malibu

Pt. Mugu State Park Boundary

Ranch Center Rd.

Sycamore Multi-Use Area

Danielson Muti-use Area

BONEY MOUNTAIN STATE WILDERNESS

Potrero Rd.

Satwiwa Cultural Center (NPS)

Wendy ↗ Walk-In

N

1 mile

Overlook Trail in Pt. Mugu State Park with Boney Mountain in the background.

Mark Langton

Valley *(currently closed to bikes)* has one of the finest displays of native grasslands left in California. Bluffs near the ocean are among the few places in the world with giant coreopsis, a small tree-like shrub with bright yellow spring flowers. Silvery sycamores, thriving on deep underground water, mark the canyon floor and put on a wild display of color in the fall.

The park is inhabited by several large animals including mountain lions. In winter, thousands of Monarch butterflies come through during their migration south from colder climes. And because Point Mugu is located on the northwest tip of Santa Monica Bay, it provides an excellent viewing point for the California gray whale migrations in winter and spring.

Four miles northwest of Sycamore Cove, an observation platform on the west side of Pacific Coast Highway overlooks the saltwater Mugu Lagoon. There is a picnic table here, and it's a good place to watch for birds. Point Mugu Rock, a popular bouldering area for climbers, is located one mile to the southeast. From the observation platform you can see several rare or endangered birds, including the brown pelican, light footed clapper rail, Belding savannah sparrow, California least tern and marsh sandpiper. To the east of the lagoon grows the giant coreopsis. Do not disturb these birds or plants; they are protected species. *Note:* The property behind the fence belongs to the Government. Unauthorized persons must stay out.

Many archeological sites from the Chumash culture have been discovered at Point Mugu State Park. Ranching began during the Spanish period when the area was known as the Guadalasca Land Grant. Most recently it was the Danielson family ranch. The Danielsons sold the land to the State to be preserved as a park. This was a critical event in the development of the Santa Monica Mountains National Recreation Area, since there were plans to develop a hotel and golf course on the Point Mugu park land. Local environmentalists joined efforts, and eventually this western cornerstone to the Santa Monicas was acquired for public use.

Sycamore Canyon in Point Mugu State Park draws big crowds. Use extra caution if you ride here, especially on summer weekends. For a more pleasant ride, we suggest cycling during the week or in winter.

Big Sycamore Canyon Fire Road

Mileage: 16.4 miles out and back with several loop possibilities.
Level of Difficulty: Generally easy with a steep climb on the north end.

From the beach side of Pacific Coast Highway, Big Sycamore Canyon fire road (also known as Big Sycamore Canyon Trail) begins at the north end of the Sycamore Canyon Campground. It winds along the bottom of deep, enclosed Sycamore Canyon through sycamore and oak groves near a seasonal stream.

0.0 mile: Entrance to the fire road at the far end of the campground. At 2.0 miles, you pass a picnic bench under a huge overhanging oak tree. At mile 3.9 is the entrance to the Wood Canyon Vista Trail, a section of the Backbone. Wood Canyon Vista Trail is a 1.8-mile single-track that climbs up to Overlook Trail. It is moderate to difficult most of the way, a good challenge to experienced riders. You may choose to descend this trail back down into Sycamore Canyon after climbing Guadalasca Trail—mile-

age markers are described later in this section.

Keep right at the Wood Canyon

Overlook Trail in Pt. Mugu State Park with La Jolla Canyon and Pacific Ocean in the background.

Mark Langton

Junction, mile 4.0. At mile 4.4 is the fire road cutoff to Ranch Center Road on the left. Keep right. At mile 4.7 is a junction with a paved road. Stay left on the pavement and watch for occasional cars. (Right leads to Danielson Multi-Use Area.) At 5.1 miles you will find water and por-tapotties. At about 5.5, keep right at the fork. Ranch Center Road (paved) goes left. Just short of 6.6 miles there is water and a California Wilderness Area trailhead signed *Closed to bikes.* Begin a steep hill. Climb to the top of the hill at a water tower at mile 7.2. The road drops down to Satwiwa Nature Center at 8.2 miles and out the Newbury Park exit.

Sycamore Canyon/Wood Canyon Loop with Guadalasca Option

Mileage: Loops of 11.4 or 13.5 miles (plus about 4 miles for Guadalasca).
Level of Difficulty: Generally moderate to difficult with moderate singletrack and one difficult climb.

Wood Canyon is a beautiful, shaded, streamside environment with abundant wildlife. This beautiful ride offers two options: an 11.4-mile loop is almost all on dirt, while the 13.5-mile trip climbs the paved but seldom-used Ranch Center Road. (At Ranch Center you can see the old ranch house, now used to house park employees.) Both rides start on the Big Sycamore Canyon fire road from the beach side of Pacific Coast Highway, climb to a water tower overlooking the Ranch Center, then follow the fire road through lush, rolling Wood Canyon.

0.0 mile: Entrance to the Big Sycamore Canyon fire road at the end of the campground. At mile 0.5 you pass Sycamore/Overlook Junction and at 2 miles there's a picnic table and an overhanging oak. Mile 4.0 marks the junction of Sycamore and Wood canyons. Bear right. Turn left at 4.4 miles onto a fire road cutoff to Ranch Center Road. (See next ride for the longer option with a bit more pavement.) This is a steep climb to a water tower at 5.4 miles and the crest of Ranch Center Road. Turn left and descend a paved, steep downhill. *Caution: There are off-camber turns, occasional cars and trucks, and loose gravel.* At the bottom of the hill, turn left through the Ranch Center at 5.9 miles (phone and portapotty available). Turn left again on Wood Canyon Road, which takes you through some exciting whoop-de-doos. *Control your speed and watch for other users. There are several blind corners here.*

Guadalasca Trail Option: At mile 7.1 you will come to the Guadalasca Trail, which used to be a ranch road. Guadalasca starts out fairly wide and groomed then narrows down to overgrown doubletrack, climbing gradually through a beautiful riparian oak forest and then gaining elevation quickly into scrub oak. At just under 8 miles a singletrack comes in from the left. Take the singletrack and begin climbing several tight switchbacks. At about 10 miles, you top out at the intersection of North Overlook fire road. Turn left up a short hill and then descend to the intersection of Hell Hill and

Overlook Trail in Pt. Mugu State Park with La Jolla Canyon and Pacific Ocean in the background.

Mark Langton

Overlook Trail just past mile 11.

Just a few yards past this intersection on Overlook Trail is the entrance to Wood Canyon Vista Trail to the left. Turn left here to descend the moderate-to-difficult 1.8-mile single-track back to Sycamore Canyon. Turn right at Sycamore Canyon to return 3.9 miles to the campground. Total mileage for this route is 16.7.

For the main route that keeps you on the ridge above Sycamore Canyon, go straight on Overlook Trail for about a mile of gentle panoramic views of Sycamore and La Jolla canyons and the Pacific Ocean. At mile 14.7 you meet Big Sycamore Canyon fire road. Turn right and ride 0.5 mile back to the campground for a total of 15.2 miles.

If you bypass Guadalasca Trail, continue down Wood Canyon. At mile 7.5 you come to Deer Camp Junction. Go left at the fork. (Hell

Hill rises at the right fork and climbs to Overlook Trail). At mile 8.3, you rejoin Big Sycamore Canyon fire road. Turn right and return to Big Sycamore Canyon Campground to exit at mile 11.4.

For a slightly longer loop with more paved road, stay right on Big Sycamore Canyon fire road at the 4.4 mile junction. Continue on the main trail to 4.7 miles and the junction with a paved road. Go left on the paved road (right is the Danielson Multi-Use Area). Just past 5.1 miles you'll find water and a portapotty.

At 5.5 miles turn left at the fork with Ranch Center Road (paved) and climb two hills to the water tower at mile 7.5. From here the ride is identical to the one above: Ranch Center to Deer Camp Junction; bear left. At junction with Big Sycamore Canyon fire road, go right. At mile 13.5 the fire road exits at the campground.

Sycamore Canyon/Overlook Trail Loop

Mileage: 9.8 miles.
Level of Difficulty: Moderate with one very steep hill.

This ride climbs to Overlook Trail and can be done in either direction. If you ride counter-clockwise, you have a shorter, steeper climb with a longer descent and better ocean views. Prior to the opening of Wood Canyon Vista Trail (part of the Backbone Trail), you had to climb Hell Hill at the base of Deer Camp Junction. Now you have the option of climbing the 1.82-mile Wood Canyon Vista Trail, a wonderful, winding single-track with canyon and ocean views. It's a little longer, but easier and more fun than climbing Hell Hill. While the line-of-sight is fair-to-good most of the way, there are still several blind corners. *Watch for bikes coming down, and be extra careful of hikers and equestrians if you are traveling down-hill on Wood Canyon Vista Trail.*

0.0 mile: Entrance to Big Syca-more Canyon fire road at the end of the campground. At mile 0.45 you pass Sycamore-Overlook Junction. (If you wish to do this ride clockwise, turn left here and reverse the following directions.) At mile 2.0 pass the picnic tables at an overhanging oak. Turn left at about 4.0 miles onto Wood Canyon Vista Trail and climb 1.8 miles to Overlook Trail. Or you can stay on Sycamore Canyon a tenth of a mile to Wood Canyon Junction on the left at 4.0 miles. Continue

to Deer Camp Junction at 4.8 miles.

At Deer Camp junction bear left and uphill to climb Hell Hill. There's a reason this is called Hell Hill. Although only 0.8 mile, it is an agonizingly steep, 16+ percent grade fire road. It is protected from the ocean breezes with eastern exposure, making it as hot as its name in the summer. At 5.7 miles you top out at Overlook Trail.

We recommend that you take Wood Canyon Vista Trail; it's 0.1 mile shorter and much easier, and you get better views. Access Wood Canyon Vista from Big Sycamore Canyon 0.1 mile before the junction with Wood Canyon. Turn left (west) on Overlook, which follows ridges down to Big Sycamore Canyon. There are great views of Sycamore Canyon, La Jolla Valley and the ocean as you head down. (Going straight leads to La Jolla Valley, *currently closed to bikes.*) To the right (east, away from ocean) is the North Overlook Trail, which climbs moderately 1.3 miles to

Overlook Trail in Pt. Mugu State Park with Sycamore Canyon and Pacific Ocean in the background.

Mark Langton

the park boundary (the last third of a mile descends) and 1.2 miles to Guadalasca Trail, affording beautiful views of the canyon below, as well as some higher elevation ocean vistas. *Caution: When descending Overlook* *Trail toward the ocean, watch for hikers coming uphill.* At mile 9.3 Overlook Trail rejoins Big Sycamore Canyon fire road. Go right into the campground and exit at mile 9.8.

RANCHO SIERRA VISTA

Access: Wendy and Potrero Roads at the Newbury Park entrance to Point Mugu State Park (see above).

Some bicyclists bound for Point Mugu leave their cars at the intersection of Wendy and Potrero and then ride a singletrack to the main Big Sycamore Canyon fire road. The Satwiwa Native American Indian Culture Center, located on the main road through Rancho Sierra Vista, is open Sundays from 9 a.m. to 5 p.m. with exhibits and informal talks on Indian life and culture as well as the early ranching activity that replaced them.

Rancho Sierra Vista Trails

Mileage: Out-and-back connectors of 1 to 2 miles.
Level of Difficulty: Easy with some moderate singletrack.

You can go directly into the park at Wendy and Potrero, or go uphill on Potrero a half-mile to a trail entrance on the right. (To the left is the parking lot for COSCA Los Robles Ridge Trail.) The singletrack trail comes back down to just below the Wendy Walk-In, paralleling Potrero. Turn left when you get to the main Rancho Sierra Vista Trail from the walk-in. At mile 0.4 you come to a Y; go right following the base of the foothill. At mile 0.6 you come to another Y and go right again. This trail takes you to Big Sycamore Canyon Road, mile 0.9. Turn left to go down into Sycamore Canyon.

Continue about a quarter mile to a gate and the Cultural Center on the left. All trails to the left are closed to bikes. However, just ahead about 50 yards is a trail that comes in from the right which takes you north and over to the main parking lot for Pt. Mugu State Park. The trail climbs steeply then follows the low hill, with the parking lot below you to your right. Follow the trail down and to the right around a large oak, then follow the trail back up as it parallels the access road out to Potrero Road. The trail from the Cultural Center to Potrero Road is approximately two miles long. It is known as Jack's Trail in commemoration of John "Jack" Short, a dedicated resident and activist.

At the time of this guide's printing the National Park Service was still under construction on their new visitor center. When completed, the access to Rancho Sierra Vista and Pt. Mugu State Park will be from Potrero Road across from the Dos Vientos community.

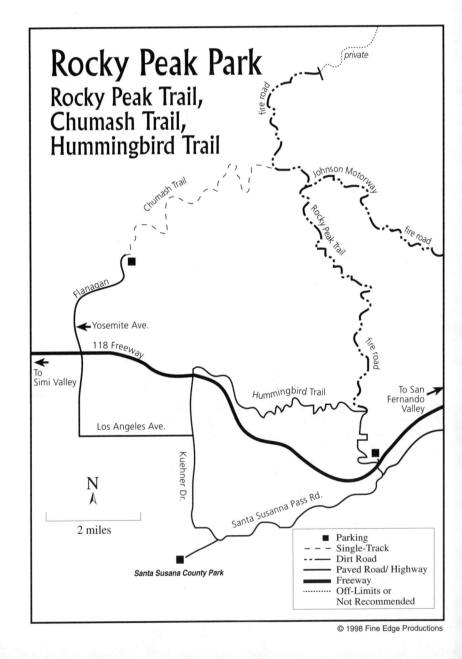

Rocky Peak Park
Rocky Peak Trail, Chumash Trail, Hummingbird Trail

© 1998 Fine Edge Productions

CHAPTER 7

Santa Susanna Mountains

Rocky Peak Park; Happy Camp Regional Park

To the northeast of the Santa Monica Mountains lies a short mountain range known as the Santa Susanna Mountains. This area, while comprised of several small parcels, is most noted for two properties administered by the Santa Monica Mountains Conservancy. The first, Rocky Peak Park, rests on the border between the Simi and San Fernando valleys. In fact, both can be seen sprawling below to the west and east from several view points along the Rocky Peak Trail. You will quickly see why it is called Rocky Peak, with its spectacular rock outcroppings and moonscape appearance. The second area is Happy Camp Regional Park in Moorpark, a lush riparian oak forest with the steep, sharp spine of Big Mountain affording expansive views of unspoiled open space.

Like many of the open areas in Southern California, the Santa Susannas were (and still are) home to large cattle ranches. As well, many locations still serve as sets for the television and movie industries. Large tracts of land are privately held, and you can often find yourself on private property if you're not careful. Please watch for fences and 'no trespassing' signs, and above all else respect private property and livestock.

While not technically in the Santa Monica range, the Rocky Peak Park and Happy Camp are close enough to the mountain biking community who use the SMMNRA and COSCA to be included here in this guide.

ROCKY PEAK PARK

Access: There are three main access points, with a fourth only accessible by bicycle because it is in a gated community. The most popular trailhead is at the Rocky Peak Road-Freeway 118 overpass at the eastern side of the park. This is

Johnson Motorway just before Rocky Peak Trail, looking south with San Fernando Valley in the background.

the main trailhead. From the east (405 freeway, San Fernando), take the 118 freeway to Rocky Peak Road exit. Parking is on the right as you come to the overpass, as is the trailhead. From the west (23 freeway, Simi), take the 118 freeway to Kuehner Drive, turn right (south) and follow Kuehner as it curves to the east and turns into Santa Susanna Pass Road. The 118 freeway will be to your left. Turn left at Rocky Peak Road and cross over freeway to trailhead.

The second trailhead is at the base of the Chumash Trail, at a lower elevation on the western side of the park. Take the 118 freeway and exit at Yosemite. Go north (uphill, away from Simi Valley) about a half-mile to Flanagan Drive. Flanagan goes up and curves to the left. Drive to the end and Chumash Trail.

The third trailhead is at the base of Hummingbird Trail, from the floor of Simi Valley at Kuehner Drive. However, this is not a recommended access point as Hummingbird Trail is best when descended. Hummingbird Trail comes off of Rocky Peak Trail. See description below.

For the fourth access point, you must ride your bike after parking your car. Known as Johnson Motorway, it is farther east than the Rocky Peak Trail. From the 118 freeway, exit at Topanga Canyon Blvd., go south (toward San Fernando Valley) to Santa Susanna Pass Road. Turn right to Iverson Drive, go 200 yards to the parking lot on left (this is overflow parking for the Church at Rocky Peak, but is okay to park in). Continue by bike up Iverson, past gate (walk-over to the left, *Rim of the Valley Trail access*), and follow road uphill to La Quilla. Then turn right, follow to Macoda, turn left to Annepe Way, turn left to Ewana Place, turn right to trailhead just a few yards. Total distance from the parking lot to the trailhead is .6 mile.

Rocky Peak Trail

Distance: 5.2 miles one way.
Difficulty: Generally easy, but hilly.

Rocky Peak Trail is technically an out-and-back fire road. However, it services three other trails that drop away from the north-south ridge; two to the Simi Valley side (Hummingbird and Chumash), and one to the San Fernando Valley side (Johnson Motorway). See below for these trail descriptions. Rocky Peak, a well-established ranching area many years ago, was privately held until 1995 when the Santa Monica Mountains Conservancy gained control. The trail offers some spectacular views of the Simi and San Fernando valleys, as well as Runkle Ranch to the north. However, you have to work for it. Starting from the 118 freeway, you will climb from 1571 feet to nearly 2700 feet in 2.4 miles to reach the high point of the trail just below Rocky Peak.

The trail is fairly relentless, offering few breaks from climbing. After reaching the summit, you still have several more steep climbs and descents to the end of the trail. At mile 3.1, Johnson Motorway comes in from the east (right); at mile 3.7, the Chumash Trail comes in from the west (left); at 5.1 the trail comes to the park boundary. Beyond is working ranch land whose owners disapprove of trespassers.

Rocky Peak Trail from Chumash goes downhill, then climbs steeply again to mile 1.0, where the trail then flattens out and begins going downhill another .4 mile to a gate. The trails past the gate are private ranch roads.

Johnson Motorway

Distance: 2.7 miles one way; connects to Rocky Peak Trail at mile 3.1 from Rocky Peak trailhead.
Difficulty: Moderate to very difficult with some very technical climbing on exposed sandstone and rocks; deteriorated doubletrack, some singletrack.

Once a wide ranch road, Johnson Motorway is now a deteriorated, rutted trail that is as technical up as it is down. If you want a quick ride that offers a lot of variety both physically and visually, this is a great out-and-back 2.7 mile trail that will test your suspension and fillings! From Ewana, take the wide road up to the first hairpin right bend at 0.2. Bear left onto the narrower, rutted trail with exposed shale and sandstone. It is a very technical and treacherous climb, so take it easy, there's lots more to come! Stay on main trail, don't take any side routes. After climbing for about a mile, you can see Oat Mountain to your right. On the other side of Oat Mountain is Santa Clarita. Continue up Johnson Motorway through amazing rock formations and several sandy washes. At 2.7 miles the trail meets Rocky Peak Trail, the main trail in Rocky Peak Park, elevation approximately 2600 feet. Ahead of you is Simi Valley. Left takes you two miles down to the Hummingbird trail, and just beyond that (0.8 mile) the 118 freeway. Right takes you 0.6 mile to the entrance to the Chumash Trail.

Johnson Motorway looking west to Rocky Peak in Rocky Peak Park.

Mark Langton

Chumash Trail

Distance: 2.7 miles one way, connects to Rocky Peak Trail at mile 3.74 from Rocky Peak trailhead.
Difficulty: Difficult to very difficult, with some very loose and technical sections.

From the trailhead at the end of Flanagan, stay on main trail as it climbs, very steeply in some places, to Rocky Peak Trail at 2.7 miles. Watch for cyclists coming down and hikers coming up. This is a great out-and-back ride, or you can combine it with Rocky Peak and Hummingbird trails.

If you use this trail in conjunction with Rocky Peak Trail from the 118 or Santa Susanna County Park, the only way to make a loop back to the Rocky

Peak trailhead (without going on private property) is to go down Flanagan to Yosemite, left to Los Angeles Street, left to Kuehner, right to Santa Susanna Pass Road, and back up to the parking at Rocky Peak. (The property to the east at the bottom of Chumash Trail is parkland for several acres next to Flanagan, but there is no egress from the property as it is private to the east. To see the system of roads and trails on the private property, head east away from the homes on Flanagan on the paved road, then branch off onto the doubletrack and up over the narrow saddle. You will see a large water tank on your left ahead. Take this dirt road another 0.5 mile to an overlook. Below you is a box canyon. If you were to take the dirt road down into the canyon and meet up with the paved road at the bottom, you could then take the paved road to a steep, rocky climb and over to another trail that connects with Kuehner. But again, this area is private property.)

Note: An option for Chumash Trail is to park at the bottom of Santa Susanna Pass Road at Santa Susanna County Park. The 2-mile pavement climb up to the Rocky Peak Trail is a good warm-up, and by doing it this way you end your ride without a climb! To get to Santa Susanna County Park, turn off Santa Susanna Pass Road where it meets Kuehner Drive onto Katherine Street and go 0.2 mile to the county park on right.

Hummingbird Trail

Distance: 2.8 miles one way from Rocky Peak trailhead to Kuehner and 118; 6.1 miles round trip using Kuehner and Santa Susanna Pass.
Difficulty: Difficult to very difficult, with some very technical sections and steep drop-offs.

From Rocky Peak trailhead and 118 freeway, the trail climbs steeply to the Hummingbird Trail at 0.8 miles (it seems a lot longer!). There's a sign post and bench. Turn left (west) and begin the fun but very technical 2-mile descent down to Kuehner. There are several steep drop-offs that come

Mark Langton

Hummingbird Trail in Rocky Peak Park, looking west into Simi Valley.

up quickly, so always be alert. Also be on the lookout for hikers coming up the trail any day of the week. At mile 1.8 you come to a weird and wonderful slickrock outcropping. At mile 2.8 you come to the bottom of Hummingbird Trail and a stream crossing. Directly to your left is the 118 freeway. You can go back up Hummingbird (mostly hiking), or continue on pavement to Santa Susanna Pass Road and Rocky Peak Trail entrance. To continue on pavement, cross the stream and bear left up the steep embankment, then across the large open lot to Kuehner Drive. Turn left on Kuehner under the freeway and go 1.1 to where Kuehner curves left and turns into Santa Susanna Pass Road. Continue up 1.9 miles to Rocky Peak Road, turn left over the freeway to the parking area.

Note: An option for Hummingbird Trail is to park at the bottom of Santa Susanna Pass Road at Santa Susanna County Park. The 2-mile pavement climb up to the Rocky Peak Trail is a good warm-up, and by doing it this way you end your ride without a climb! To get to Santa Susanna County Park, turn off Santa Susanna Pass Road where it meets Kuehner Drive onto Katherine Street and go 0.2 mile to the county park on right.

HAPPY CAMP REGIONAL PARK

Big Mountain Trail

Distance: 12.9 miles round trip.
Difficulty: Moderately difficult loop, sandy and rutted in places, with some steep sections.

Access: From Thousand Oaks/Ventura, take the 23 freeway north to New Los Angeles Avenue/Princeton Avenue, turn left onto Princeton Avenue. From San Fernando and Simi Valleys, take the 118 west to New Los Angeles Avenue/Princeton Avenue, turn right onto Princeton Avenue. Take Princeton to Campus Park Drive. The entrance to Happy Camp is another quarter mile up Campus Park Drive, but there is no parking along this stretch of Campus Park Drive or at the park entrance. You can either park on the side streets near the entrance, or in the parking lot of the mini-mall at the corner of Princeton and Campus park.

Happy Camp Regional Park is managed by the Eastern Ventura County Conservation Authority, a joint powers agency of the Santa Monica Mountains Conservancy and County of Ventura. Located in the western Santa Susanna Mountains, it consists of 3000 acres of riparian oak habitat with year-round running water. It was home to several Chumash Native American groups and later supported the immense Strathearn Ranch. There are still many signs of ranching such as watering troughs and other equipment.

Happy Camp has only a couple of routes: an out-and-back canyon ride along an oak lined ranch road, or a loop route that consists of a fairly

Entrance to Hummingbird Trail from Rocky Peak Trail in Rocky Peak Park.

Mark Langton

Chumash Trail, Rocky Peak Park.

Mark Langton

substantial climb and ridge trail that drops back into the Happy Camp Canyon several miles up canyon. There are several spur access roads off the canyon bottom starting at about mile 5, but these quickly become steep and rutted, leading to wire towers and private property. They're fun for exploring, but no loops are available legally.

Starting at the entrance gate, ride the paved gravel road 0.7 mile to Middle Ranch Road, bear left at the Y and go another 0.2 mile to a T. Turn right (going left takes you into sandy conditions that are usually unrideable). At mile 2.3 you come to the beginning of the Happy Camp Canyon Nature Trail. (To do just Happy Camp Canyon out and back, bear left. The main canyon continues approximately another 7 miles.)

For the ridge route up Big Mountain, proceed past the info kiosk at mile 2.3, go 50 yards to fork and bear right heading uphill. This hill is fairly gradual, but can be very sandy and rutted in places. At mile 3.8 the trail tops out and begins following the ridge. To the right are the Simi hills and beyond that, Westlake Village and Oak Park. To the left is Oak Ridge

and beyond that the town of Piru.

The trail continues another 2.1 miles along the rolling ridge of Big Mountain. The last half-mile of this 2-mile stretch has a couple of steep rollers. At mile 5.9 you will begin descending a hill; in front of you will be oil rigs on a narrow promontory. At the bottom of this hill at about 6.0 miles, the Happy Camp Canyon connector trail comes in from the left. (One mile past this trail the park property ends at oil company property). Use caution going down the connector trail as it is very steep in places and can be very rutted. At mile 7.0 you reach a meadow with several large oaks, an old water tank and pump, as well as some horse hitching posts. Just past 7.0 miles, you come to the main canyon trail. (If you go right, there is another mile one-way of increasingly steep canyon riding to the park boundary).

Begin descending on the Happy Camp Canyon trail. Be careful of wash-outs and sandy sections. At mile 10.5 you return to the info kiosk where you began the climb up Big Mountain. Follow the dirt and gravel roads back to the main entrance at Campus Park, 12.9 miles round trip.

Appendices

IMBA RULES OF THE TRAIL©

Thousands of miles of dirt trails have been closed to mountain bicycling because of the irresponsible riding habits of a few riders. Do your part to maintain trail access by observing the following rules of the trail:

1. RIDE ON OPEN TRAILS ONLY. Respect trail and road closures (ask if not sure), avoid possible trespass on private land, obtain permits and authorization as may be required. Federal and State wilderness areas are closed to cycling. Additional trails may be closed because of sensitive environmental concerns or conflicts with other users. Your riding example will determine what is closed to all cyclists!

2. LEAVE NO TRACE. Be sensitive to the dirt beneath you. Even on open trails, you should not ride under conditions where you will leave evidence of your passing, such as on certain soils shortly after a rain. Observe the different types of soils and trail construction; practice low-impact cycling. This also means staying on the trail and not creating any new ones. Be sure to pack out at least as much as you pack in.

3. CONTROL YOUR BICYCLE! Inattention for even a second can cause disaster. Excessive speed maims and threatens people; there is no excuse for it!

4. ALWAYS YIELD TRAIL. Make known your approach well in advance. A friendly greeting (or bell) is considerate and works well; startling someone may cause loss of trail access. Show your respect when passing others by slowing or even stopping. Anticipate that other trail users may be around corners or in blind spots.

5. NEVER SPOOK ANIMALS. All animals are startled by an unannounced approach, a sudden movement, or a loud noise. This can be dangerous for you, others, and the animals. Give animals extra room and time to adjust to you. In passing, use special care and follow the directions of horseback riders (ask if uncertain). Running cattle and disturbing wild animals is a serious offense. Leave gates as you found them, or as marked.

6. PLAN AHEAD. Know your equipment, your ability, and the area in which you are riding, and prepare accordingly. Be self-sufficient at all times, keep your machine in good repair, and carry necessary supplies for changes in weather or other conditions. A well-executed trip is a satisfaction to you and not a burden or offense to others. Keep trails open by setting an example of responsible cycling for all mountain bicyclists.

FUNDAMENTAL MOUNTAIN BIKE SKILLS

by Mark Langton

There's no substitute for time in the saddle or for experiencing the wide variety of terrain that mountain biking has to offer. However, there needs to be a basic understanding of the fundamental skills in order to progress and become a really accomplished rider. The following techniques will introduce you to many of the basics that are needed to ride a mountain bike off-road.

Basic Starting and Stopping—Because a trail can often be uneven, you should never start or stop on the saddle. *Starting:* Straddle the bike with one foot on the ground and one foot on either pedal, with the pedal at two or ten o'clock, so you can get a good push as you pedal the first revolution. Push on the "up" pedal as you raise up and back onto the saddle. (You will need to have the bike in a gear that allows you to raise up without the pedal coming around too fast.) DO NOT "SCOOT" THE BIKE FORWARD WITH THE FOOT THAT IS ON THE GROUND! As the other pedal comes around, place your foot on top of it immediately. Do not look at it; keep your head up and look ahead. Get at least two or three revolutions going and some momentum before you try to put your foot into the toe clip or clipless pedal.

Stopping—As you slow the bike down (both brakes at the same time), put your pedals at six and 12 o'clock, slide forward off the saddle as you place your weight on the "down" (six o'clock) pedal, and slowly brake to a stop. Just as you are about to come to a complete stop, remove your "up" (12 o'clock) foot from the pedal, lean slightly to the side of the up foot, slide forward off the saddle, and place the up foot on the ground, coming to a complete stop.

Cadence—Your most efficient revolutions per minute (cadence) is 60-80 rpm. Not too fast and not too slow. Remember, you are trying to be efficient. Use your gears often to maintain a consistent cadence.

General Seated Riding Position—The basic position for riding on relatively flat terrain, while seated, is with the waist bent, arms bent slightly and elbows rotated inward slightly, not sticking out. This allows the arms to rise and fall with the front tire when going over bumpy or rolling terrain while pedaling seated. (Never lock your elbows. Locked elbows make the arms and shoulders rigid, which delivers shock to the neck and head. While locking the elbows may feel comfortable, it is ultimately more tiring because the head and neck get jostled excessively.)

An additional technique while riding in the saddle is to lean forward into the bike when encountering a sudden rise in terrain, then rising slightly off the saddle while pedaling to let the rear tire roll over the rise.

Crouch—For downhilling and negotiating obstacles with momentum and pedals level: stand up with even pressure on both pedals and butt off the saddle; knees are slightly bent, waist bent so thighs are gripping the rear of the saddle, and arms bent and firm but relaxed. Two fingers (middle and index) are on the brake levers at the ready or braking at the same time (do not grab the brakes hard; instead pump or "feather" them so you don't skid the tires on loose dirt). Picture a jockey or off-road motorcycle rider.

Remember to let your arms bend as the front tire goes over the obstacle (hits the bump). The faster you're going or the steeper the hill, the more you need to bend your waist and let the front of the bike come up to you by bending your arms. Also, remember to keep your weight rearward (thighs against the wings of the saddle) to lighten the front tire so your weight is not thrown forward. DO NOT PUSH YOUR WEIGHT REARWARD BY STRAIGHTENING YOUR ARMS! Only in the steepest of conditions do you need to get this far back behind the saddle.

Cornering—Always use both brakes at the same time. If the turn is smooth, use the One Leg Down technique (inside pedal is up, leg bent; outside pedal is down, leg straight). If the turn is rough or steep, use the crouch (see above). You can also use a combination of the One Leg Down technique and the crouch depending on the terrain. One portion of the turn may necessitate a crouch, while the latter part may allow you to get one leg down. If you are using the One Leg Down technique, you can also counter-steer (negative lean). Instead of leaning the bike into the turn, force the bike to a more vertical (upright) position as you lean your shoulder into the turn slightly. This keeps the contact patch of the tires more stable and prevents the tires from slipping on loose gravel or sand. Remember to keep the upper body low (waist bent) and arms relaxed and bent. Do not sit upright as it makes your center of gravity higher and takes weight off the front tire. Weight on the front tire is necessary to maximize traction in the dirt.

Carving Turns—This is an outgrowth of the negative-lean style of turning. If the terrain is smooth and free of loose rocks or sand, you can *lean the bike into the turn,* keeping your body more vertical, rather than leaning your body into the turn and keeping your bike more vertical. As the bike leans over, push the handlebar into the turn (for example, if you are turning left, move the handlebar and lean the bike laterally left, into the turn). You can use this technique both in the crouch (off the saddle) and seated. You must relax your arms so that the bike can move over the terrain freely and you have more control with your arms. Relax your arms up and down (vertically), and side-to-side (laterally). If you use this technique while seated, combine it with the One Leg Down style (outside leg down, pedal at six o'clock; inside pedal at 12 o'clock).

Scanning—Always look ahead far enough so you can plan your next two "moves" (the next two things you need to do to keep going), as well as directly in front of your front tire for specific obstacles you need to avoid. For example, on a wide fire road with good sight distance, your scan can be far ahead; on a tighter trail with lots of obstacles, your scan is much shorter. ALWAYS LOOK WHERE YOU WANT TO GO, NOT WHERE YOU DON'T WANT TO GO. FOCUS ON THE GOOD LINE, NOT ON THE BAD LINE.

Don't Attack the Bottom of the Hill—Maintain a steady and even pace at the bottom of the hill, shifting into a gear that allows you to pedal smoothly and consistently up the majority of the hill. Save a little bit for the top of the hill. If you feel you have some extra energy and can see the top, shift up to a harder gear. Remember, if you have to slow down at the top to recover, you may as well have left it in the gear you were in.

If you stand up out of the saddle to relax your back or gain a little power, shift a maximum of only one or two gears. You want to maintain your cadence relatively close to what it was when you were sitting and spinning. Remember that your cadence may be well below 60 rpm on steeper hills, so shifting to a harder gear may take quite a bit of effort to maintain when standing. When out of the saddle on a steep hill, only pedal for approximately 10 revolutions, as more can tire you out. You need to match the seated cadence and standing cadence with your heartrate. In most cases, seated and spinning is more efficient.

The classic "crouch position": pedals level, butt off the saddle, inner thighs hugging the rear part ("wings") of the saddle, waist and arms bent.

Transition Hill Climb—Use your momentum to help you shift gears smoothly as you transition from a downhill to an uphill. Shift your gears early when there is less pressure from your legs working against the chain and derailleurs. Try not to shift under heavy leg pressure; use it only as a last resort.

Short-burst Hill Climbing Out of the Saddle— This technique is used when coming from a downhill or higher-speed flat section and you are familiar with or can see the top of a short hill. It allows you to stay in the gear you're in and use momentum and power, rather than shifting into a lower gear and pedaling seated. As you get to the first part of the hill, use your momentum to find a comfortable gear to "power climb" the remainder of the hill. As the grade of the hill starts to slow you down, shift your hands to the bar ends (if you have them), lift up off the saddle and pull from side to side on the handlebar, rocking the entire bike from side to side. Bend your waist and upper body deeply into the bike to get maximum benefit from pulling on the handlebar.

Steep Hill Climbing—To compensate for rearward weight transference as the hill gets steep, move forward on the saddle approximately 1-2 inches, bend forward, pull back toward your hips with your arms (down on the handlebar, not to your chest), keep elbows in and pull with your arms with each pedal stroke (pulse rhythmycally).

Hovering—This is used to reduce shock to the body from the rear tire over small bumps. *Crouch*: Stop pedaling just before bump, rise up briefly as you pass over bump. *One Leg Down:* Stop pedaling just before bump, stay in saddle with one leg down, raise your body up off saddle slightly and bend forward slightly, putting pressure on the down leg to lighten your weight on the saddle. *Pedaling:* Same techniques as the Leg Down, except you keep pedaling as you traverse the bump. Stay in saddle as you pedal, bend forward slightly, raise up off saddle slightly just as the rear tire rolls over the obstacle.

Ratcheting (slow speed maneuvering)—This technique is very effective for riding around or over obstacles on the trail when you are going slowly. Keep your body low (waist bent) to minimize the bike being top heavy and wanting to fall to the side. As you approach the obstacle, you want to be in a gear that is easy enough so that you can pedal quarter revolutions—from two o'clock to four o'clock—with the outside foot (the foot to the outside of the turn, if you are turning). Steer toward the outside of the turn, rather than the inside, as the rear tire draws a tighter radius than the front in tight turns. As you reach the exit of the turn, you can resume full pedal revolutions.

Slow Speed Technical Maneuvering—Climbing: Feel the terrain under your tires and be aware of how much power you are giving to the rear tire. You can't just power through the section. You need to throttle the torque to the rear wheel so that you don't spin the tire. You also need to have your fingers on the brake levers to slow you down if you start to go off your line. Be sensitive to how your butt is lifting off the saddle to let the rear tire track and follow the undulations of the terrain.

Descending: Again, feel the terrain under your tires by feathering the brakes. You can't simply have the brakes on at one pressure, you must pump them (let off, get back on) constantly. Remember: even when the terrain doesn't look threatening, you still need to get your chest down into the bike (bend the waist and arms, keep your head up scanning the terrain) and be relaxed over the bike.

Slow Speed Log Hopping—Using your slow speed maneuvering technique, approach the log (or other high obstacles) and do a quick power wheelie to get the front tire up and onto the log, and to give you momentum to carry your bike over the log. You need to be in a gear low enough that when you push hard on the pedals, the front tire comes up 1-2 feet as you travel forward. You can assist the front tire's rise by pulling firmly on the handlebar as you push quickly and firmly on the pedal. If you're in the correct low gear, you need only about half of a pedal revolution for this action. Start this technique with the power stroke of the pedal, not pulling on the handlebar.

As soon as the front tire is on or over the log, lift up off the saddle and get the rear tire up to the log. If the log is so high that the big chainring hits, you can either pedal the crank using the chainring to dig into the log and power your bike over, or you can lunge the bike using an upward and forward lunging motion, aided by your toe clips or clipless pedals.

Rut Crossing, Descending—Always try to cross a water erosion rut as soon as you encounter it. The longer you wait, the more likely it is to get deeper, wider, and harder to cross. Look for a shallow section where the far edge is least angular. Use the Crouch position, cross the rut at as sharp an angle as possible. (If you go into the rut at a relatively parallel angle, your front and/or rear tire will not be able to climb out the other side.) Do not use your front brake as your front tire rolls over and through the rut. Apply your brakes as necessary only after your front tire rolls over the rut. Keep your butt off the saddle until the rear tire has cleared the far edge of the rut.

Starting Uphill and Downhill—*Uphill*: With both brakes on, lean the bike over to get onto the saddle, then get the bike completely vertical (no lean) as you sit on the saddle. Look for a rock or high spot of dirt and put one foot there to help you balance. Assume the uphill climbing position. You must remember not to push too hard when starting so you won't spin your rear tire (you'll be in an easy gear and it is easy to spin the tire when starting on a hill if you give too much pressure to the pedals). If you can get 3 pedal revolutions going, you're on your way. Remember to keep your weight forward and arms pulling rearward, not up to your chest. *Downhill*: With both brakes on, lean the bike over to get onto the saddle, then get the bike vertical as you sit on the saddle. Keeping your weight back, slowly release the brakes (but not all the way) and get into the crouch position immediately.

Stopping on a Steep Hill—*Downhill*: Keeping your weight back and your body in a crouch, come to a stop, or slow enough so that you can put one foot down as you lean the bike over. Do not move forward of the saddle. Keep your weight over the saddle or the rear of the bike will come up because you are braking so heavily. If the trail is wide enough, steer across the face as if you were skiing across the fall line; then come to a stop, putting your foot out and leaning the bike into the hill. *Uphill*: Because of the pitch of the hill and height of the saddle, it can be difficult to put your foot down on a steep uphill. Find a high spot on the trail for your foot, or steer across the face (if the trail is wide enough) and lean the bike into the hill as you put your foot down.

Switchbacks—*Downhill*: Get into your crouch (weight back and arms steady, feet up), steer toward the outside of the turn, then turn sharply back the other direction. Hang your rear end away from the saddle and toward the outside of the turn at the mid-way point. As you begin feeling gravity take you out of the turn and downhill, drop your outside foot to six o'clock and your inside foot to twelve, pedaling if necessary to get you out of the turn. You may even have to come to a complete stop to negotiate the turn, so you'll need to backpedal (ratchet) slightly to get yourself going out of the turn. *Uphill*: As you enter the switchback, steer to the outside of the turn, keeping your arms firm and your shoulders square. As you reach the apex of the turn, lean the bike into the turn laterally with your arms, keep your body upright, scoot forward slightly on the saddle, pull rearward with both arms, and apply pressure to the pedals sparingly but firmly. Don't pedal too hard or your front tire will wash out or come off the ground entirely. You may want to be in a gear that's slightly higher (harder) than the one you were using, as you want less torque going to the rear tire when in the switchback. If you can't change the gear, *remember to back off on the power to the pedals.*

ACCESS POINTS TO THE SANTA MONICAS

The following parking areas are listed east to west. Reference numbers are the page and grid numbers in *The Thomas Guide, LA County Street Guide and Directory, 1992,* except for Chapter 6, which refers to their Ventura directory. However, any good Los Angeles street map will show most of the parking sites. Where there are 2 references given, the first number refers to *Thomas* guides prior to 1992. The second page number refers to *Thomas* guides later than 1992.

Ref. #

CHAPTER 1

Griffith Park: Travel Town—Forest Lawn Dr. & Griffith Park Dr.	563:H:4
Greek Theater—2700 N. Vermont Avenue	593:J:1
Fern Dell—Western & Fern Dell	593:H:2
Lake Hollywood Reservoir—Lake Hollywood Drive	563:E:7
Laurel Canyon, Fryman Canyon Overlook— 8400 Mulholland Drive	592:H:1
TreePeople—Coldwater Canyon & Mulholland Drive	562:F:7
Franklin Canyon—Ranger Station	562:F:7 and 592:F:1
Wilacre Park—Fryman Road and Laurel Canyon	562:G:7

CHAPTER 2

East Side of Dirt Mulholland—Mulholland and Encino Hills Drive	561:D:7
Mountaingate and Sepulveda Boulevard—West Side Los Angeles	591:F:2
North end of Kenter Avenue	591:E:7
Mandeville Canyon and Gardenland Road	591:C:2
North end of Westridge Road	591:C:7
Northwest end of Queensferry Road	631:C:1
Northwest end of Casale	631:D:3
Trailer Canyon and Michael Lane	590:F:7
North end of Paseo Miramar	630:G:4
San Fernando Valley—Encino Hills Drive and Mulholland	561:D:7
South end of Reseda Boulevard	560:H:6
South end of Gleneagles (Van Alden)	560:F:7
South end of Winnetka	560:E:5
South end of Natoma	560:D:6
South end of Canoga	560:B:5
Topanga Canyon Boulevard—Trippet Ranch Park Headquarters on Entrada	590:C:6
East end of Cheney Drive	590:D:3
North end of Santa Maria Road	560:D:6

CHAPTER 3

Summit Motorway and Old Topanga Road	589:G:1
Red Rock Road	589:G:4
Stunt Road and Calabasas Peak Motorway	589:E:5

Ref. #

CHAPTER 4
Malibu Creek Park Entrance—south of Mulholland and
    Malibu Canyon/Las Virgenes   588:G:5
Malibu Creek Park Entrance—Liberty Canyon entrance   588:E:2
Mesa Creek Motorway at Tapia Park   628:H:1
Puerco Canyon & Pacific Coast Highway   628:F:7
Corral Canyon Parking Lot   628:B:1
Solstice Canyon/Latigo Backbone Trail—Corral Canyon   628:B:1
Solstice Canyon/Latigo Backbone Trail—Kanan-Dume   627:D:1
Lakeside Lateral   588:A:5 and 587:J:5
Crags Drive   588:B:5
Cheeseboro Park—main entrance at Chesebro Road   558:D:5
Palo Comado Canyon—Doubletree/Sunnycrest
    (Ventura Guide)   558:B:1
King James Court/China Flat via Dead Cow (Ventura Guide)   527:H:6
Paramount Ranch   588:B:3

CHAPTER 5
Zuma Ridge/Zuma Canyon—Parking pullout on Kanan-Dume   667:F:2
North end of Bonsall Drive   667:D:1
North end of Merrit Busch Drive   627:D:7
Encinal Canyon & Buzzards Roost Sign   587:A:6
Charmlee County Park—Park entrance on Encinal Canyon   626:F:3-4
Circle X Ranch—Park headquarters or upper parking lot
    (Ventura Guide)   585:H:4, J:3
Rocky Oaks Park   587:D:6
Brewster Motorway   587:E:5-6
Newton Motorway, Latigo Canyon at Hellacious Acres   627:D:1

CHAPTER 6
All from Ventura Guide
Point Mugu State Park—Main entrance on
    Pacific Coast Highway   81A:B:6 *(old)* 387:A:4 *(new)*
Pinehill Road & Potrero Road   555:E:4
Potrero Road & Dos Vientos   81:E:3 *(old)* 555:D:4 *(new)*
Rancho Sierra Vista—Wendy Drive & Potrero Road   555:F:5
Los Robles Canyon—Potrero Road parking area   555:H:4
Moorpark Road   556:E:2, F:2
Fairview Road (Westlake Open Space)   557:A:3
North Ranch Open Space (Pathfinder)   527:G:6, G:7
North Ranch Open Space (Hillcrest)
Tamarack Road   557:A:5
Lake Sherwood   556:H:6
Wildwood Park—Arboles parking lot   526:B:2

Ref. #

CHAPTER 7
Coordinates refer to Ventura County Thomas Guide   (old/new)
Rocky Peak Road/118 freeway   67:F:1/499:F:3
Flanagan Road (Chumash Trail)   57:C:4/479:B:6
Iverson Road (Church at Rocky Peak)   6:B:1 (Los Angeles)/499:H:2
Kuehner Drive & 118 freeway   57:D:6/499:C:1
Santa Susanna County Park
   (Katherine & Santa Susanna Pass)   67:D:2/499:C:4
Princeton & Campus Park   54:D:3/476:H:6

Rogers Road Trail in Topanga State Park, just north of Will Rogers State Historic Park, looking toward downtown and West Los Angeles.

AGENCIES AND ORGANIZATIONS
WITH PROGRAMS
IN THE SANTA MONICA MOUNTAINS

California Department of Parks and Recreation (CDPR)   (818) 880-0350

California Native Plant Society   (818) 348-5910

Conejo Recreation and Parks District (CRPD) (805) 495-6471

Conejo Open Space Conservation Agency   (COSCA) (805) 449-2100

Concerned Off-Road Bicyclists Association (CORBA)   (818) 773-3555

Equestrian Trails Inc.   (818) 367-1401

Fire Closure Info: (805) 488-8147

Los Angeles City Recreation & Parks Department   (213) 485-5555

Los Angeles County Department of Parks and Recreation (LADPR)
(213) 738-2961

Malibu Creek Docents   (818) 706-8809

Moorpark Parks and Recreation   (805) 529-5092

Mountain Bike Unit   (818) 882-2839

National Park Service (NPS)   (818) 597-9192 or (805) 370-2300
401 W. Hillcrest, Thousand Oaks, CA 91360

Rancho Sierra Vista/Satwiwa   (805) 375-1930

Rancho Simi Recreation and Park District   (805) 584-4400

Sierra Club   (213) 387-4287

Santa Monica Bay Audubon Society   (310) 478-8846

Santa Monica Mountains Conservancy (SMMC)   (310) 589-3200

Santa Monica Mountains Trails Council   (818) 888-9830

Save The Mountain Park (STMP)   (818) 348-5910

Small Wilderness Area Preservation   (818) 246-1493

Topanga Canyon Docents   (818) 888-6856

Topanga-Las Virgenes Resource Conservation District   (818) 455-1030

TreePeople   (818) 769-2663

Trips For Kids   (818) 882-2839

William O. Douglas Outdoor Classroom   (310) 858-3834

Will Rogers State Park Docents   (310) 454-8212

Wilderness Institute   (818) 887-7831

MOUNTAIN BIKE EQUIPMENT CHECKLIST

BEFORE YOU RIDE:

☐ *PROPERLY ADJUSTED MOUNTAIN BIKE*—See BIKE CHECK below.

☐ *HELMET*—Properly fitted; square on head, not tilted back; straps must meet under ears; chin strap must be tight enough so you cannot completely open your jaw.

☐ *WATER*—8-16 ounces for every 30-60 minutes, depending on heat and exertion level.

☐ *GLOVES*—Protect hands over rough terrain and in the event of a fall. Also absorb moisture for better control of the handlebar.

☐ *CYCLING SHOES*—Solid pedaling platform, better tread for walking/hiking.

☐ *SHORTS*—Absorb perspiration and reduce chafing; longer and tight so material won't get in the way of saddle.

☐ *UPPER BODY CLOTHING*—Close-fitting, wicking material to better evaporate perspiration (avoid baggy T-shirts or sweatshirts as they can snag on branches or saddle; cotton stays wet and can contribute to hypothermia in extreme cases). For cooler weather, dress in layers, and always carry a windbreaker.

☐ *EYE WEAR*—Protects against branches, bugs and dust.

☐ *TOOLS*—Minimum of chain breaker, Allen (hexagonal) keys, tire lever/Quik Stick, new innertube and/or patch kit, mini-pump.

☐ *HIGH CARBOHYDRATE SNACK*—If riding more than two hours. (If fructose intolerant, try using trail mix consisting of nuts and raisins or other dried fruits such as dried apricots).

☐ *FIRST AID*— Gauze, adhesive bandages, antibacterial cream, cloth tape, bandanna, antiseptic wipes, sting ointment, space blanket, medical info, emergency contacts, identification, blood type, etc.

☐ *SUNSCREEN*—Especially on neck, ears, and backs of arms and legs.

BIKE CHECK

☐ *CLEAN*—Cleaning regularly can help you spot trouble before it gets serious. Use low-pressure garden hose or spray bottle. Do not use high-pressure wash. Bio-degradable degreaser on chain/drivetrain. Take your bike to your dealer as part of your service warranty.

☐ *DRIVE TRAIN LUBRICATION*—Clean and lube every 2-4 rides, preferably with light viscosity lubricant.

☐ *BRAKES ALIGNED*—Make sure brake pads are not rubbing tire and are contacting rim surface correctly and completely.

☐ *CABLES/WIRES OKAY*—Check for fraying or unraveling wires, and worn, cracked or broken outer cables.

☐ *PROPER TIRE PRESSURE*—40-60 pounds per square inch (psi) depending on rider weight. See sidewall for psi range info. (Rider weight/psi examples: 130 pounds/35-40 psi; 175 pounds/40-50 psi; over 200 pounds/50-60 psi.)

☐ *QUICK RELEASE POSITION*—Feel tension at 90 degrees, close with palm of hand. Should be pointed tip UP.

FIRST AID

by Réanne Douglass

Several years ago on a mountain biking trip, I miscalculated a sharp turn on a sandy stretch of dirt road, went flying and turned my right shin into raw meat. I didn't have a first aid kit with me. Why bother? After all, I was cycling off-road, no traffic around, and I planned to be gone just part of the day. When I got home, I took a shower, cleaned my wound and applied some antibiotic cream. Three days later, Don had to carry me to the doctor. A staph infection—that took three pain-filled weeks to control—had set in.

Don't be careless like I was. Carry and use a First Aid Kit. You can purchase one at bike shops or sporting goods stores, or you can make your own. For day rides, we suggest taking the following items:

8 Bandaids 1" x 3"	8 Aspirin Tablets or Aspirin Substitute
6 Antiseptic Swabs or 1 oz. Hydrogen Peroxide	8 Gauze Pads 3" x 3"
1 Roll Adhesive Tape	1 Elastic Bandage
1 Moleskin 3" x 4"	1 Needle
1 Single-Edge Razor Blade	Waterproof Matches (in film can)
Sunscreen 15 SPF or more	Prescription Medicine (if applicable)
	4 Antacid Tablets

SELECTED REFERENCES

BOOKS

Day Hikes in the Santa Monica Mountains
Santa Monica Mountains Task Force
Sierra Club, Angeles Chapter, 3550 West Sixth Street, Los Angeles, CA 90020

Day Hikers Guide to Southern California
John McKinney
Olympus Press, P.O. Box 2397
Santa Barbara, CA 93120

Flowering Plants of the Santa Monica Mountains Coastal
& Chaparral Regions of Southern California
California Native Plants Society
6223 Lubao Road, Woodland Hills, CA 91367

Hiking in Topanga State Park
Milt McAuley
Canyon Publishing; 1980
8561 Eatough Avenue, Canoga Park, CA 91304

Hiking Trails of the Santa Monica Mountains
Milt McAuley
Canyon Publishing; 1981
8561 Eatough Avenue, Canoga Park, CA 91304

Mountains to the Sea
A Visitor's Guide to the Santa Monica Mountains and Seashore
Santa Monica Mountains National Recreation Area; 1983
National Park Service, 30401 Agoura Road, Agoura Hills, CA 91301

MAPS

Santa Monica Mountains Mountain Biking Map
with ride descriptions and trail profiles
Fine Edge Productions
Route 2 Box 303, Bishop, CA 93514

The Thomas Guide
Los Angeles and Ventura Counties Street Guide and Directory; 1991,
and 1992 (new format)
17731 Cowan Street, Irvine, CA 92714

Topographic Maps
United States Geological Survey
Federal Building, 300 N. Los Angeles Street, Los Angeles, CA
(800-USA-MAPS)

Trails of the Santa Monica Mountains
California Coastal Trails Foundation, 1986
P.O. Box 20073, Santa Barbara, CA 93120

ROUTE INDEX

Baleen Wall Trail   *61*

Big Mountain Trail   *115*

Big Sycamore Canyon Fire Road *103*

Boney Mountain/Backbone Trail
  to Carlisle Canyon   *81*

Bulldog Loop, Lakeside Lateral
  Loop/Lookout Loop   *50*

Butte Trail/Santa Rosa Trail
  Loop   *95*

Canyon Overlook Trail   *61*

Castro Crest, Newton and Brewster
  Motorways   *52*

Charmlee Natural Area County
  Park   *79*

Charmlee Trails   *79*

Cheeseboro Canyon Park   *58*

Chumash Trail   *112*

Circle X Ranch   *81*

Conejo Crest Loop,
  White Horse Canyon Trail,
  Triunfo Park Trail   *86*

Corral Canyon/Mesa Peak/
  Puerco Canyon   *52*

Crags Road   *50*

Cross Mountain Park   *23*

Eagle Rock/Eagle Springs Loop   *37*

East Side Dirt Mulholland   *27*

Edison Road into Zuma Canyon   *75*

Franklin Canyon Pavement
  Climb   *25*

Gardenland to Westridge   *29*

Grasslands Trail   *49*

Griffith Park   *21*

Happy Camp Regional Park   *115*

Happy Hollow Campground and
  the Grotto   *81*

Hollyhock to Mandeville Canyon   *29*

Hummingbird Trail   *113*

Johnson Motorway   *111*

Kenter Fire Road   *30*

Lake Hollywood Reservoir   *22*

Las Virgenes Trail   *49*

Liberty Canyon Trail   *48*

Loop Trail/Creek Trail/
  Pond Trail   *77*

Los Robles Canyon and Los Robles
  Ridge Trail   *88*

Los Robles Canyon Open Space   *88*

Lynnmere Trail from Lower
  Wildwood Canyon through
  Arroyo Conejo   *94*

Lynnmere Trail Loop from
  Arboles Parking Lot to
  Wildwood Canyon   *95*

Magic Forest Trail   *25*

Malibu Creek State Park   *45*

Modello Trail   *61*

Mountaingate/Mandeville   Canyon
  (Kenter) Fire Road   *29*

Natoma Fire Road   39

North Ranch Open Space   96

North Ranch Open Space Trail—
    Sandstone Hills Trail, Hillcrest
    Open Space Preserve   98

Palo Comado Access/Lower Palo
    Comado Canyon Loop   62

Palo Comado Canyon,
    China Flat, and Oak Canyon
    Regional Park   63

Palo Comado Canyon/
    China Flat/Oak Park Loop   65

Paramount Perimeter Trail   69

Paramount Ranch   69

Paseo Miramar   36

Phase II Trails   71

Picnic Overlook in TreePeople   25

Point Mugu State Park   100

Puerco Canyon and Mesa Peak
    Motorway   53

Rancho Sierra Vista   107

Rancho Sierra Vista Trails   107

Red Rock/Calabasas Peak   43

Reseda to the Hub   36

Rides from Westside Los Angeles   30

Rocky Oaks   76

Rocky Peak Park   109

Rocky Peak Trail   111

San Fernando Valley to the
    Mountains   36

Solstice Canyon/Latigo/Zuma
    Canyon Backbone Trail   53

Sulphur Springs Trail/
    Sheep Corral   60

Sullivan Canyon Trail   32

Sullivan Ridge Fire Road   32

Summit Motorway   43

Sycamore Canyon/Overlook
    Trail Loop   106

Sycamore Canyon/
    Wood Canyon Loop with
    Guadalasca Option   104

Temescal/Trailer Canyons   38

Topanga State Park   40

Trailer Canyon   36

TreePeople to Franklin Canyon   23

Trippet Ranch/East Topanga
    Loop   40

Westlake Open Space   85

Westridge Fire Road   31

Wildwood Canyon Loop via
    Lizard Rock   93

Wildwood Mesa Trail, Stagecoach
    Bluff Trail, Lizard Rock
    Trail   93

Wildwood Park   91

Will Rogers State Historic Park/
    Rogers Road Trail (Backbone
    Trail)   33

Zelzah Fire Road   30

Zuma Canyon   73

Zuma Ridge Motorway   74

Outdoor Publications from
Fine Edge Productions

RECREATION TOPO MAPS FROM MOUNTAIN BIKING PRESS™
(with Mountain Biking, Hiking and Ski Touring Trails,
6-color, double-sided, includes trail profiles & route descriptions)

Eastern High Sierra-Mammoth, June, Mono, 2nd Ed., ISBN 0-938665-21-9	$9.95
Santa Monica Mountains, ISBN 0-938665-23-5	$9.95
San Bernardino Mountains, ISBN 0-938665-32-4	$9.95
San Gabriel Mountains—West, ISBN 0-938665-13-8	$8.95
North Lake Tahoe Basin, 2nd Ed., ISBN 0-938665-34-0	$8.95
South Lake Tahoe Basin, 3rd Ed., ISBN 0-938665-35-9	$8.95

Laminated copies – $10 additional

MOUNTAIN BIKING GUIDEBOOKS FROM MOUNTAIN BIKING PRESS™

Mountain Biking Southern California's Best 100 Trails, 2nd Ed., Fragnoli & Douglass, Eds., ISBN 0-938665-53-7 (classic routes, 80 detailed maps, 352 pages)	$16.95
Mountain Biking Northern California's Best 100 Trails by Fragnoli & Stuart, ISBN 0-938665-31-6 (classic routes, 80 detailed maps, 300 pages)	$16.95
Mountain Biking the Eastern Sierra's Best 100 Trails, by Hemingway-Douglass, Davis, and Douglass, ISBN 0-938665-42-1	$18.95
Mountain Biking Santa Monica Mountains' Best Trails, by Hasenauer & Langton, ISBN 0-938665-55-3	$14.95
Mountain Biking North America's Best 100 Ski Resorts by Fragnoli, ISBN 0-938665-46-4	$16.95
Mountain Biking the San Gabriel Mountains' Best Trails with Angeles National Forest and Mt. Pinos by Troy & Woten, ISBN 0-938665-43-X	$14.95
Mountain Biking South Lake Tahoe's Best Trails by Bonser & Miskimins, ISBN 0-938665-52-9	$14.95
Mountain Biking North Lake Tahoe's Best Trails by Bonser & Miskimins, ISBN 0-938665-40-5	$14.95
Lake Tahoe's Top 20 Bike Rides on Pavement & Dirt by Miskimins, ISBN 0-938665-36-7	$6.95
Guide 4, Ventura County and the Sespe, 3rd Ed. by McTigue, ISBN 0-938665-18-9	$9.95
Guide 10, San Bernardino Mountains by Shipley, ISBN 0-938665-16-2	$10.95
Guide 11, Orange County and Cleveland N.F., 2nd Ed. by Rasmussen, ISBN 0-938665-37-5	$11.95
Guide 13, Reno/Carson Area by Miskimins, ISBN 0-938665-22-7	$10.95

OTHER GUIDEBOOKS

Up the Lake With a Paddle, Canoe & Kayak Guide, Vol. 1, Sierra Foothills, Sacramento Region, by Van der Ven, ISBN 0-938665-54-5	$18.95
Favorite Pedal Tours of Northern California, by Bloom, ISBN 0-938665-12-X	$12.95
Ski Touring the Eastern High Sierra, by Douglass & Lombardo, ISBN 0-938665-08-1	$8.95

To order any of these items, see your local dealer or order direct from Fine Edge Productions. Please include $2.50 for shipping with check or money order. California residents add 7.25% tax.

MOUNTAIN BIKING PRESS™

FINE EDGE Productions

Route 2, Box 303
Bishop, California 93514
Fax (760) 387-2286
Prices are subject to change.
© 1998 Fine Edge Productions

www.fineedge.com